The Remarkable Aileen Coleman

The Desert Rat

by

Annette Adams

Foreword
by
Franklin Graham

Cover photograph by Russ Busby

Huntington House Publishers

Huntington House Publishers
P.O. Box 53788
Lafayette, Louisiana 70505

PRINTED IN THE UNITED STATES OF AMERICA.

Library of Congress Card Catalog Number 2001099335
ISBN 1-56384-193-2

Cover Photo by Russ Busby

Dedicated to my daughter,

SUSIE ADAMS MOORE,

who has always been

but a phone call away

with loving encouragement.

Contents

Foreword

Through our earthly pilgrimage we find ourselves meeting certain individuals who stand out and make a significant impact in our lives. Aileen Coleman is one such person who made a distinctive impression on my life. I was eighteen when I first met this tall, slender woman. She walked with a kind of cocky swagger, and I couldn't help but notice her.

There was something uniquely different about this individual. As a missionary to the desert kingdom of Jordan, it looked as though she just didn't fit. She had a crazy sense of humor and an infectious smile. But she also had a spirit of determination that God used to move mountains.

I have seen Aileen hard at work and hard at play. I have also seen her serving the humble, meek, and lowly. I have seen her in the audience of kings and princes.

Her life has made an impact not just on my life, but on a nation and a people. How in the world could a lady from the Outback of Australia turn her world—the Arab world—upside down?

I believe her story will rivet you. When all is said and done you will realize that God's Hand is on the wheel of life. This remarkable woman has been a light in a dark world and is an example of what God can do with a life sold out to Him. He has done it with Aileen, and He'll do it with you.

I trust her story will be a blessing and encouragement—a motivating force in your life.

Franklin Graham
President, Samaritan's Purse
September 1999

photo by Dennis Schulz

Aileen Coleman

"The Desert Rat"

"The Desert Rat"

by

Annette Adams

An "angel of the desert"—
Her admirers named her that.
But ask her what she calls herself,
You'll hear "the desert rat."

She's so much like the rest of us—
Her needs, her loves, her heart;
But, observing her *in action*
Is what sets her far apart!

Success to her is not numbers—
Big crowds of humankind.
It's healing, loving Bedouins,
That "one lost sheep" she'll find.

So:
I long to tell this story—
I'm about to "tip my hat"
To this "Angel of the Desert"
That she calls "The Desert Rat!"

Acknowledgments

I have had so many helpful people in my life, who, over the years, through their love, have been participants in this enterprise—too many to name. However, the following have played especially important parts in helping to see this project through to its completion:

Jeanne Patterson, creative writing professor at Palomar College, who, in response to a one page biography assignment, was the first to suggest that I write this book—and more importantly, led me to believe that I could.

Dennis Schulz, journalist/photographer from Australia, who graciously gave permission for me to use quotations and photographs from his *Qantas In-Flight* magazine article, entitled, "Angel of Mafraq" (May-June 1991).

Mr. and Mrs. Clarence Severt, daughter and son-in-law of Lester Gates, who contributed valuable photos and information relative to the chapter on him.

The Coastline Community Church of Solana Beach, California, and its Pastor, James Christoferson, who generously supplied my husband with the magnificent computer which encouraged this household to write.

Dr. Lane G. Adams, my spouse, who has served as a tireless typist, sounding board, cheerleader, and 'in-residence' errand-boy.

Mr. Paul Bremner, our good friend, whose computer expertise and patient counsel preserved both the manuscript and the mental health of the above mentioned typist. Mrs. Kathleen Bremner, Paul's wife, who suggested we contact Huntington House Publishers at Vital Issues Press.

And to Mark Anthony, Kathy Doyle, and Theresa Trosclair, (Publisher, Managing Editor, and Marketing Director of Huntington House), for their enthusiasm and guidance in the publication of this work of love.

Ashley Moore, my granddaughter, whose excellence in grammar and punctuation has been of such great assistance.

Franklin Graham, President of Samaritan's Purse, for his longtime support and leadership in promoting the ministry of Aileen Coleman and the Annoor Hospital, and for writing the foreword.

Introduction

Consider the character of a woman, a registered nurse with a master's degree in Arabic, who, with another female, a physician, enters a Moslem land in 1965. By 1973, with no visible means of financial support, she and the doctor have built a completely equipped sixty-bed hospital just outside of Mafraq, Jordan. In an environment hostile to both her sex and her Christian religion, this miracle of mercy was accomplished.

She started out looking very much the Australian-born college girl she was. She had a tall, willowy frame that bespoke great potential for modeling, and large, beautiful eyes set in a face whose bone structure begged to be photographed. Over forty years later, dressed in Bedouin garb, she could easily be mistaken for a stalwart Bedouin woman. Lines of love and service have been deeply etched into her face by the sun, wind, and desert dryness. It is a winsome weathering brought on by a lifetime of devotion to God and a heartfelt compassion for the suffering of the Bedouin people. However, after you've been around her for a while and experienced her great sense of humor and exuberant vitality, an inner beauty comes forth that tends to obliterate what time, suffering, and service have done.

She's a healer, who herself has been healed from tuberculosis, from a serious siege of cancer, and, most recently, from a near-fatal auto accident. She is stoic in her own sufferings, while showing utmost tenderness to others in pain. What a rare combination she is: strong, but not hard.

She has never married and yet has raised at least nine infants, either abandoned by their parents because of a hopeless condition, or handed over because of the death of the mother. I have answered the phone many times through the years to hear tearful requests for prayer for her sick babies. She didn't just nurse these children back to good health; she truly bonded deeply with each one, and they with her. It tore me up to know how much she cared because I knew that, inevitably, she would have to face the greatest test of all—the return of the healthy child, a few years later, back to the tents as their culture demands.

She has been made a "blood brother" in a completely male-dominated Bedouin tribe, and is called "A`raisa" by one and all. It means "The Leader." She has been honored by both Queen Noorah of Jordan and Queen Elizabeth of England. She has the title of Dame Aileen Coleman throughout the British Commonwealth. When *Qantas Airlines In-Flight* magazine put her picture on the cover, they called her "The Angel of the Desert." She calls herself, "The Desert Rat."

After the completion of this manuscript, the world experienced the tragic death of His Majesty, King Hussein of Jordan. The text assumes at every place that this great leader is still alive. I ask the readers to make the appropriate mental adjustment as they read.

Special Update

Americans went into shock on September 11, 2001, when ultra-radical extremists of the Islamic religion used hijacked American airliners as kamikaze missiles to attack the World Trade Towers in New York and the Pentagon in Washington DC. An outpouring of outrage over this barbaric act came not only from the nations of non-Islamic faith, but also from many of the Islamic nations as well. In Amman, Jordan, ordinary Moslem citizens made up lines, up to a mile long, waiting to sign a Book of Mourning to be sent to the United States expressing their grief and outrage over this act. King Abdullah expressed a similar response.

In the pages of this book you will encounter the grass roots story of a miraculous fact: That in the Middle East, where violence and hatred smother and burst into flame from day to day, there is an oasis of love where Christians have loved Moslems, serving profound medical needs among the Bedouins; and, in response, Moslems have loved Christians in tangible ways, even to the point of assisting materially in the work.

At the heart of this story is Aileen Coleman. I have tried faithfully and honestly to communicate in these pages the reality of this wonder, which is still going on at this hour.

Annette Adams

Receiving Award from Queen Noor, King Hussein's wife, 1990

Receiving Order of Australia from Queen Elizabeth II, delivered by her emissary, the Governor General of Australia, in Canberra, 1990

Receiving Award for Service to the Community from Princess Basman, King Hussein's sister, 1994

Representing the Muslim World during a "Windows On The World" Conference, Black Mountain, North Carolina, 1996

Chapter One

The Heart of the King Is in the Hand of the Lord

I can't remember what time of day the telephone call came. The date was 25 February 1996. On the other end of the line was the carefully controlled voice of Dr. Eleanor Soltau, thoracic physician, and longtime medical missionary to tubercular Bedouins in the Middle East. The trauma-tinged tone of her voice let me know up front that something was terribly wrong. The call was coming from Amman, Jordan.

"Annette," she said, "she's going to make it, but I wanted you to know that Aileen was in a horrifying automobile crash with two of her fellow missionaries as passengers. All three are here at Medina Hospital.

"As they were pulling out on to an expressway, their car was hit on the driver's side by a drunk whose speed was estimated to be somewhere around one hundred miles per hour. Aileen has multiple injuries: eight broken ribs, a punctured lung and kidney, a broken arm, crushed pelvic bones, and shattered lumbar vertebrae.

"Your visit here, planned for March, will have to be postponed." In the background I could hear a weak voice saying: "Tell them to come on anyway." It was a typical response from the pioneer heart of Aileen Coleman, my dear friend, registered nurse, hospital administrator, evangelist, and longtime partner of Dr. Eleanor Soltau.

Later I was to learn something very remarkable, something that touched me deeply. Aileen's very special Jordanian friend, Princess Zein, had been seen by her cousin, King Hussein, as she sat outside Aileen's hospital room. (Don't confuse King Hussein with Saddam Hussein of Iraq. The king was there, visiting patients in this military hospital.) He inquired as to why the princess was weeping. After she'd related the terrible news of the accident to him, he expressed great sorrow and said, "Send the hospital bills to me."

It was then, more than ever before, that it began to dawn on me what an amazing impact these two Christian women have had in this Moslem land. Even the king himself knew of their merciful ministry of healing and compassion to his beloved fellow Bedouins. A direct descendant of Mohammed, grandson and successor to his grandfather, King Abdullah demonstrated royal generosity and concern for this servant of Christ in absorbing the cost of this tragedy. But there was more of his generous regard yet to be shown.

Later on, when my husband wrote a letter of thanks to the king for the utter kindness he had shown to Aileen, our understanding of the esteem in which he held her was vastly expanded. Who expects an answer from a busy king, ruling in the midst of the most explosive part of the earth? But answer he did, with a most amazing personal letter. We'd never seen one written in this way before. The greeting was in his handwriting, while the body of the letter was typed. The farewell and the signature were once again in his own handwriting. The delivery was special to us as well. It came to us by mail from the Jordanian Ambassador in Washington, D.C. with his personal card attached. Inside the very large envelope was another large flat envelope with the king's seal in wax. It had obviously been hand-carried to Washington, and from there posted to us.

The letter contained a personal invitation from the king for us to be his guests for our entire time in Jordan. It also contained an encouraging report on the recovery of Aileen Coleman, plus an expression of gratitude for my husband's letter and a hope that he would be able to personally greet us when we arrived. Of course we recognized at once that this amazing invitation had nothing to do with us, and everything to do with his regard for the life and ministry of Aileen Coleman. The king's gracious actions brought to mind the verse in Proverbs 21:1, which says, "The heart of the king is in the hand of the Lord. He directs it like a watercourse wherever He pleases." As for Aileen and Eleanor, these events confirm their fulfillment of another verse which states, ". . . that your daily [lives] may win the respect of outsiders" (1 Thess. 4:12a).

In November of that same year, we did tour Jordan as the guests of the king. Aileen insisted on being our guide, although pain had remained her constant companion since that terrible car crash. The entire trip was "fairy-tale" memorable—from the time we were met at the Allenby Bridge by two of the king's chauffeur-driven Mercedes-Benz cars (one for baggage and one for us) to our return in the same grand manner eight days later. We were met by two handsome, young palace aides, accompanied by Aileen. After a warm welcome by one and all, we and our luggage swept through customs and immigration more rapidly than we had ever experienced before in all our travels.

We were driven up out of the Jordan Valley to Amman, where accommodations at the Intercontinental Hotel were awaiting us. The palace had also, thoughtfully, provided a room for Aileen in order that we might spend all of our visit with our dear friend. We had the same driver for the whole exciting time. He was a lieutenant in the army, smartly uniformed, wearing a beret and carrying a hip-holstered pistol. He escorted us to all the best restaurants, and all the historic and scenic sites which had been very thoughtfully preplanned for us by the king's assistant chief of protocol. And most importantly, we finally saw that which we had heard about and been praying for all these years—The Annoor Tuberculosis Hospital.

The Annoor Tuberculosis Hospital is in the north near the Syrian border and is located just outside the village of Mafraq. It is surrounded by productive olive groves, orchards, and gardens. What a welcome contrast is the verdant green of the hospital compound to its desert environment.

The hospital was immaculately clean. But somehow its obvious sterility did not keep it from feeling comfortable, welcoming and warm. I was very impressed and touched by the friendly, smiling faces of the patients. Although we were there at a rest time for the children, they let us visit their ward anyway. They must have been expecting us—at least we felt that way—because as we walked in, they were sitting up in their beds, and each little face lit up with a smile that I can still shut my eyes and see. What happy excitement! What a heartwarming reception! A little later on, after their rest period was over, the children caught up to us and gave us a joyous impromptu concert of a number of Christian songs they had learned from the staff in the hospital. It would have been impossible to program a performance like theirs. It was sheer enjoyment. They all had the most dazzlingly deep, dark eyes. Their faces ranged from fascinating to absolutely beautiful.

We also visited the women's wards. They, too, had those captivating eyes. Some of the little mothers were breathtakingly lovely, but often their tired, tattooed faces had begun to look far older than their years. This premature aging had been caused by a combination of childbearing at a very early age and the hardship of their primitive life-style in the desert tents. That, along with the ravages of disease, uncared for until their admission to the hospital, contributed to early aging. (The statistics there show the opposite from our country: generally speaking, the men live longer in their culture.) But the women all exhibited friendliness and cheerfulness, and had such lovely smiles. Aileen says they are not complainers like we have a tendency to be in the West. They remain positive under the most difficult circumstances. She said their buoyant, carefree manner touched something deep inside her from the start, and that one has to admire their great sense of independence and pride.

The name of the hospital, Annoor, means "The Light," and I sensed an aura of "light" that accompanied us as we walked through the wards of the hospital. It is seen not only on the faces of those who staff the hospital, but it is reflected on the countenances of the patients as well. Jesus Christ said, "I Am the Light of the World. He who follows Me shall not walk in darkness, but have the light of life" (John 8:12). It is as if God Himself is smiling in a special way on this mission of mercy.

As we were being treated to this tender tour of healing and happiness, I couldn't help but think of Jesus' words, "Inasmuch as you have done it unto the least of these My brethren, you have done it unto Me" (Matt. 25:40).

We were also able to see their outpatient clinic at Ras A Naqab, which is 185 miles to the south. It is near the small town of Ma'an, and the famous, ancient carved city of Petra. It is located on the top of a mile-high mountain with a view that takes the breath away. What a joy it was to behold these two oases of physical and spiritual healing in this otherwise barren and bleak desert. A former police station and jail about one hundred yards from the clinic will soon be remodeled into a very small hospital that will be able to house inpatients as well. All that is wanting is funds to finish it, and personnel to staff it.

As we began our sight-seeing tour we were staggered by the incredible beauty of Jordan. Among the biblical and historical sites that shall be forever etched in my memory are: the top of Mount Nebo, the amazing city of Petra—carved out of pink and multicolored rock, the extraordinary magnitude of the observable ruins and amphitheaters of Jerash, and the eerie mystery of the Crusader castle perched on the top of the mountain at Ajlun.

At Mount Nebo, one of the most overwhelming views of the Jordan Valley, the Dead Sea, and the mountains of the Promised Land can be seen. This is the place where Moses stood for his farewell address to the children of Israel. (Because of his previous disobedience to God, he was not allowed to lead the children of Israel into the Promised Land.) The day we were there was quite cold, cloudy, and windy, with occasional showers. While we stood there posing for Aileen to take a picture, the sun broke out directly over the city of Jerusalem, and for a brief moment, we could see why ancient pilgrims called it "Jerusalem the Golden."

Perhaps the most thrilling thing to see on the top of Mount Nebo is a stunning sculpture that looks, at first glance, like a simple cross. Upon closer examination one can see that it is the fulfillment of the Scripture in John 3:14-15 that says, "Just as Moses lifted up the snake in the desert, so the Son of Man must be lifted up that everyone who believes in Him may have eternal life." A wire serpent is twisted around the vertical upright of the cross, and the crossbar itself is shaped to look like the arms of man, limp in death. The part above the cross is clearly a man's head, cast slightly forward in a death position, and the wire body of the serpent is in the shape of a halo, surrounding this Sacred Head. It is obvious that this is Jesus Christ on the cross just at the moment of His death. The entire symbolism is spelled out in 2 Corinthians 5:2, which says, "God made Him who had no sin to be sin for us, so that in Him we might become the righteousness of God."

The overwhelming aspect of this to me is that here in a Moslem land, looking across to the modern Jewish state of Israel, stands this towering symbol of the life, death, and resurrection of Jesus Christ. It gives me chills to think about it. (I'm also gripped with a deep sadness to recall that such a symbol would no longer be legally permitted to stand on state-owned property here in the United States.) But there it stands in Jordan. Praise God.

When our days in Jordan came to an end, we were taken out to dinner as guests of Princess Zein. It warmed my heart to see her obvious affection and respect for Aileen and her enthusiastic support of the work of Annoor Tuberculosis Hospital. It's also wonderful to know that this most attractive, sophisticated, American-college-educated princess, and member of the royal Hashemite family, dons Bedouin garb with Aileen and treks out into the desert to minister to her fellow Bedouins. Imagine the impact on the tent-dwelling Bedouins who see their princess coming out in searing heat or bitter cold to join with "A'raisa" to meet their most basic health and human needs.

Each day as we returned from our exciting journeys, we'd receive a phone call from the assistant chief of protocol, inquiring about our day's activities and how we had enjoyed them. Late on the last afternoon, she visited us at the hotel, delivering personal gifts from his majesty as mementos of our visit. (The king was out of the country the entire time we were there, celebrating his sixtieth birthday as the guest of Queen Elizabeth in London.) To Aileen he gave a personally inscribed wrist watch, and to us a lovely small silver casket with his signature and royal seal engraved on the lid.

All the time we were there, I felt like I was somehow part of a wonderful fairy story which I hated to see come to an end. But end it did, and quite abruptly. We were royally returned to the Allenby Bridge in the king's cars, just as we'd entered. But as soon as we had crossed over the Jordan River, an Israeli cab driver impatiently hustled us into his waiting taxi, tossing our helpless baggage unceremoniously on to the top of the cab. He then made a 180 degree turn so fast that it catapulted some of our luggage off the top of the cab, skidding it along in the desert dust. We had to yell at him to stop, indicating what had happened. Disgruntled, as though the whole event was our fault, he got out, heaved the bags back onto the top of the cab, got back in, and roared off in a cloud of dust. I turned to my husband and said, "I do believe our 'Cinderella carriage' has turned back into a pumpkin."

But that did not mar our memories in any way. After that last afternoon, when we had been presented with those sweet gifts—the "icing on the cake"—I can still hear Aileen's words: "Now you can understand why we love our king, and why we are so proud of him."

It was obvious that the king had enormous regard for Aileen, as well as great gratitude for her many years of compassionate ministry to his beloved subjects. And I am still overwhelmed by the fact that King Hussein extended this amazing hospitality to us simply because he knew we were good friends of Aileen Coleman.

Her story begs to be told.

Annoor Hospital, outside Mafraq, Jordan

Ras A Naqab Clinic, near Ma'an, Jordan

The author and Aileen as the guests of PrincessZein at dinner in Amman, Jordan, in November of 1996, the last evening spent in Jordan

The sculpture on the top of Mount Nebo, Jordan, overlooking the Jordan Valley with Israel in the distance

Chapter Two

Here Am I, Send Me

I met Aileen in 1968. My husband, Lane Adams, then an associate evangelist with Billy Graham, was leading his first tour to the Holy Land. Roy Gustafson, also one of Dr. Graham's associates and an experienced tour leader, had invited missionaries to meet us at every stop to speak of their work in that particular area. He had informed us that the missionary to meet us in Lebanon was coming from Jordan. She would arrive at the hotel in Beirut on the same day our tour did. Upon checking in at the desk, we inquired as to whether Aileen Coleman had arrived. The desk clerk informed us that she had. Then she added, "I think she's in the beauty parlor getting her hair done." I hadn't even met her, and I liked her already.

She spoke to our group, exciting us with their work and their vision. Afterward, I talked to her for a while. Then I really knew I liked her! I was immediately struck with her courage, her intelligence, and her strength, all mixed with a charming vulnerability. I admired her work ethic, her unpretentious godliness, her great sense of humor, and her candor. I knew then that she was a very special lady, and our thirty years of friendship has verified this truth.

Indeed, I found her personal qualities so compelling that I have always sought to be with her as frequently as opportunity has afforded. It's always a spiritual lift for me to warm my heart at the fire which burns in hers. This is not to say that she's some sort of religious robot who gets wound up every day to perform perfectly. No, she's a real person who is sensitive enough to suffer from personal hurts, and who sometimes gets tired, discouraged, lonely, and angry just like the rest of us. But no adversity damages her relationship to Him; she always manages to bounce back, never losing sight of her Savior or her call. And when I hear of the remarkable things God is doing in her life of ministry, my own faith is always emboldened and strengthened.

Needless to say, given the distance between the U.S. and Jordan, a lot of our communication has been by letter, phone, e-mail, or fax but each visit with her has been treasured. Her departures have always left me with an aching void.

She would say she's ordinary. I'd have to say she's a good example of God taking something ordinary and making something spectacular out of it. She would say she's nothing special. Then, I would say her life is the perfect example of what "nothing special" looks like when it's sold out to being obedient to God's will.

Who is this wondrous woman? Where did she come from? And when did this love affair with the almost-unknown-to-us nomadic Bedouin people of the desert begin?

She was born in Bundaberg, Southern Queensland, Australia, in 1930, the youngest of seven children. Her father was a certified public accountant. Her mother, as can be expected, was a full-time homemaker. Aileen always loved sports—particularly swimming. She's quick to tell you that the way in which she learned how to swim was most unique—if a bit harrowing. Her older brothers took her out in a boat, tied a rope around her waist and threw her into the water. She swam. End of story . . . except to say she did win many swimming competitions later in life, during her college years. She was a nonconformist from the start—an individualist with an independent spirit. She said she might even call herself rebellious as a youth, but she'll settle for "adventurous." God was not the moving force in her life during those early years. Or rather, she was not aware of it.

Then, one night, on a dare, she attended a tent meeting during her college years in Bundaberg. She was, surprisingly, almost stunningly, reached by the message, drawn by the invitation to receive Christ, and went forward to make a commitment. She went forward to the platform all right, but went nonstop straight out the back of the tent to her dormitory. However, God did begin to powerfully move in her life, even changing her original career choice from teaching to nursing. So clear was the new direction that she entered nursing school even though her father disapproved of this new direction.

After college she attended nursing school, then Bible college. It was during her second year of Bible college that she was given an assignment to write a paper on mission work in the Muslim world of the Middle East. While doing research for the paper, the school received a letter from Dr. Sarah Hosman, an obstetrician, who was involved in a healing ministry in Saudi Arabia. Dr. Hosman asked the student body to pray for the work there. She also requested special prayer that God would send a registered nurse, with postgraduate studies in obstetrics to fill a great need they had. So Aileen began to pray fervently for both needs to be met. While praying, she began to realize that she had all the requirements necessary to answer the call herself. To her astonishment, she ended up being the answer to her own prayers. She was like Isaiah who heard the voice of the Lord saying, "Whom shall I send? And who will go for us?" And Isaiah answered, "Here am I, Lord. Send me" (Isa. 6:8).

During her Bible college years Aileen had met an attractive young man, a fellow student, with a clear call to a life of ministry. The relationship deepened into love, and engagement to be married followed. But as they contemplated a life of ministry together, this new and insistent call of God to the Muslim world in Aileen's life, was not matched by the call felt by her intended. Deep soul-searching and prayer followed, but the more they prayed the more certain each felt that their individual calls were sending them into separate pathways. With aching hearts, but with no regrets, the engagement was broken, and they followed the leading of God into completely different directions.

Though she was swept up in a very busy life, filled with the responsibility of meeting the needs of others, there were, yet, basic needs that went unanswered in her own life. As ripping as choosing the call of God over the invitation of marriage had been, it did not mean that this initial decision silenced forever the constraint of those needs. On two separate occasions, romantic relationships cried out for the consummation of marriage. Each instance involved fine, young, attractive Christian Arab preachers. As compelling as each subsequent invitation of matrimony was, and as deep as her own needs proved to be, the knowledge of the unusual cultural restraints that would be placed upon her—even in a Christian marriage—indicated to her that she had to continue to follow the singular call of God. Even in her more mature years, there was the occasion of a persistent American business man, whose amorous insistence continued over a period of two years, though such attention was not encouraged nor reciprocated.

Endless days—even though filled with meaningful work—never can fulfill the yearnings created by personal loneliness. Having gone through those experiences at such a deep emotional level might have left some people bitter and cynical. Or it might have left them envious of others who did decide to marry. Instead, one finds Aileen with no evidence of regret, but with a bright sense of humor about it all (grateful she doesn't have to make those "wretched double beds") and a complete yieldedness to life as she finds it. And, approaching those years where a treasured lifetime companion becomes even more precious, there's an almost blithe unconcern in Aileen's demeanor as she aggressively ventures forth into "the Golden Years."

So, in 1955, having initially settled the call of God, and in answer to her own prayers, she headed out to a primitive, underdeveloped Arabian village called Sharjah. It is located near Bahrain, in the Persian Gulf. (Primitive then; it is quite developed by oil riches now.)

Her first introduction to the Arab world was, to put it mildly, tough. These were tedious times of testing. Her schedule consisted of delivering babies all day and through the night. I asked her when she slept, and she said, "Between contractions." The complicated and desperate cases were the only ones brought to the hospital. The local people had a fundamental mistrust of these foreigners. The hospital was looked on by most as the last resort, when the primitive methods had failed, or worse, had served to increase the danger to mother and child.

Aileen said it was an unbelievable cycle of misery and death. They were constantly trying to undo the damage caused by the medieval practices prevalent in the Middle East at that time. A first baby would be born usually when the mother was in her early teens, and it would be delivered by a native midwife in the tents out in the desert.

Following the prevailing custom, shortly after the delivery, the young mother's vagina would be packed with rock salt to stop the bleeding. The pain that accompanied that practice goes beyond the capacity of words to express it. There was no anesthesia in the desert—nothing to take any of the screaming edge off the very worst of it. The long-term results of this horror was to form such hard scar tissue, like cartilage, that upon delivery of the woman's second child, all elasticity would have departed from the tissue, nearly preventing any appropriate dilation when labor began.

When this situation confronted the staff in the hospital they had to cut the cervix open in order for the baby to be born. Hemorrhaging followed with a touch and go battle ensuing to stop the bleeding in order to save the mother's life. (Often, a woman would have been in labor for days before she was even brought to the hospital.) One nurse would put pressure on the aorta to give Aileen time to sew up the lacerations.

In some instances, even the most radical efforts failed, and the mother bled to death. On one occasion the combination of a low hemoglobin level, caused by malaria and extreme lacerations, caused by the birth, left one and all helpless as the patient bled to death.

After watching this happen the first time, Aileen fled from the operating room sobbing and exclaiming that she couldn't take it any longer. An older missionary came to her in the depths of her misery and said gruffly, "Why did you come out here? Don't you want to help these women? If you don't, who will?" Though it hurt severely at the time to hear those words, in retrospect Aileen considers that "straight talk" a turning point in her life of service. She didn't quit. With a firm resolve, she continued on. And on, and on, and on!

She had many other difficult experiences in Sharjah. One in particular was a dark drama, indeed. When Aileen first arrived in the Arab world, an older female doctor was in charge of the hospital. She had contracted typhoid fever, and was in a very critical state. She was the only available doctor, not only in the hospital, but also in the entire vicinity.

At this time a woman was brought into the hospital who had been in labor for six long days. (As previously mentioned, only the most serious cases were brought in to the hospital.) It was apparent that if this poor suffering woman did not receive immediate attention, she would die. Examination showed that the baby was in a breach position and could not, or would not, be born. The patient was utterly exhausted and drained of everything but agonizing pain.

The diagnosis called for an immediate cesarean section operation—a procedure which only a medical doctor could perform. Aileen had assisted the doctor in a number of such procedures, but she had never even thought of doing one herself. She immediately rushed to the bedside of the ailing doctor, telling her of the situation, and protesting that there was no way she could do the procedure. The very thought of it was terrifying.

The ailing old doctor calmly said to her, "This lady is dying. If you don't try to help her, she will die. If you do try, she may die, but then again, she might live." Aileen said, "When I knew she was not going to be there with me, the thought became terrifying." But, with the old doctor's straightforward exhortation, she went back to the operating room to try to help this desperate little mother.

The doctor had a large surgical atlas that showed each step in the C-section procedure. Aileen said, "I had the book set up in plain view, and assigned a nurse to turn the pages. I read and cut, and read and cut, and instructed the nurse when to turn to the next page. I was still terrified and extremely tense as I followed the directions page by page. After what seemed like an eternity to me, the baby was finally delivered, alive and kicking. While others attended the healthy babe, I continued to follow the instructions on closure, page by page, until the C-section procedure was complete. Mother and baby were fine, and there were no complications.

I was swept with an internal explosion of gratitude to God, and blessed relief beyond words. There before my eyes was a live, healthy baby, and an utterly weary young mother. She was desperately weak, but definitely alive, with every indication of full recovery."

"But, Aileen," I said, "given the absence of trust that the people had for modern medicine, what in the world did they say when they learned that you had done the operation, not the doctor—and that you had had to follow a book in order to know what to do?" She laughed and responded, "Because we knew how they felt, we always invited one of the family members to come into the operating room, stand quietly in the corner and observe everything that we did. So there was a family member in the room during the whole procedure." "And, what was their reaction?" I queried. "Actually," she responded, "when I was completing the suturing process, I heard the family member rush out to the rest of the family to tell them the good news. 'Mother and baby are both fine,' she said. But the thing that so impressed her was that I, being a woman, could read, and she boasted, that I had done everything exactly as it was written in the great book." From then onward, Aileen was known among the Bedouins as, "The Doctorah who does everything 'by the book.' " By any standard, this courageous woman gives the term, "doing it by the book," a whole new meaning.

From Sharjah she answered a call to the Baraka Tuberculosis Hospital in Bethlehem, which was then part of the nation of Jordan, but later was annexed into Israel after the "Six-Day War" in 1967. One of the attractive features about this position was Bethlehem's proximity to Jerusalem, where Aileen could study at the University of London's extension program. Her purpose was to achieve a Master's Degree in Arabic, which she accomplished prior to the move to Mafraq, Jordan, in 1965. She proved extremely gifted in Arabic. She loves the language and is so adept in its use that most Arabs think that it is her native tongue.

Once, when we were in Jerusalem together at the entrance to the Garden of Gethsemane, a group of Arab children surrounded us with outstretched hands, shouting "Baksheesh! Baksheesh!" Before we could respond to their begging, Aileen lit in to them with a barrage of Arabic words.

The children were stunned, having thought her to be just one more tourist. Turning to an enthralled cab driver observing this scene, I said, "What is she saying to them?" He responded, "She's reminding them of all of the great Arabian contributions to the knowledge of the world, and telling them that they are shaming their ancestors by begging." Then he added, "I was born and raised in Jerusalem, and she speaks better Arabic than I do."

About this time the kids figured they'd had enough and took off at a dead run. A bit later, one of the boys, pointing at Aileen in the distance, said to some other children, not subject to her lecture, "Look out for the tall one. She looks American, but she's really an Arab, and she'll slay you with her tongue." She is rarely that threatening, but always that impressive with the Arab people.

When we lived in Houston, Texas, for the year of 1992, we lived in a high-rise apartment building near the Galleria. There were a number of young Arab men who were employed at the front desk or worked for security. When she startled them by speaking to them in perfect Arabic, they were in awe of her. They said she sounded like one native born to the language. Exhibiting typical Arabian hospitality, they immediately invited her to their homes for a meal and to meet the rest of their families. Aileen admits that she now thinks in Arabic and translates back into English. (I was curious to know if she dreams in Arabic. The answer is "yes.")

I am continually amazed at her verbal flexibility. When she is in the States she reverts back to English so smoothly. Only occasionally will she blurt out something in Arabic, or fish around for some English word that comes close to a thought, or feeling, which she insists, can be said so much more colorfully in Arabic. I am also impressed with the poise and comfort she exhibits, whether in her Bedouin surroundings or western culture. She truly has mastered Paul's statement, "I have learned the secret of being content in any and every situation . . . whether living in plenty or want" (Phil. 4:12). She is as much at home in her Bedouin garb as she is "model-like-stunning" in her western clothes and makeup.

During her eight years of ministry in Baraka, Bethlehem, she discovered an even deeper respect and love for the Bedouin patients. She describes the Bedouins as proud independents—true sons of the desert. She found that they have a delightful sense of humor, and that, although the men "run the show," they can laugh at themselves as well. While quite upright in many ways, they can lie charmingly and unashamedly. In accordance with their Muslim beliefs, she has found the Bedouin men to be very moral sexually. (She is always saddened when she returns to the States, to see that so many here are either banning, breaking, or ignoring our God's Ten Commandments.) I had a pleasant surprise when we were walking down a main street in Amman, Jordan, one night. I was window shopping, not looking where I was going. I almost bumped into a handsome, young, Jordanian man who was coming out of one of the shops and did not see me. As we almost touched, he jumped backwards, throwing both hands up in the air as though someone had just shouted "stick 'em up." It was a unique experience for me, and I stood there, stunned, wondering what had happened. He offered an apology in Arabic, and moved on down the sidewalk. Aileen explained, "According to the Koran, a man is not allowed to touch any woman other than his mother, his sister, and his wife." I was impressed with this young man's conscientious obedience to his law. I began to see why Aileen loves these "sons of the desert."

She told me that very early in her ministry, one of the Bedouin men who had received Christ as Saviour and Lord was thrown into jail because of his new-found faith. He was beaten, threatened, and half of his head and mustache were shaved off in order to force him to renounce Christ. In spite of the fact that the shaving of his head and mustache was viewed as the ultimate humiliation, he stood firm. Aileen said she visited him in jail. While there, he told her that he was at the end of his rope and that he could free himself by repudiating Christ. She looked at him with tears in her eyes, and said, "Remember, He died for you." Even after further torture and incarceration, he stood firm and eventually was released.

One cannot help but wonder, given those same circumstances, how many of us would take that kind of a stand for Jesus Christ? However, there is comfort in the comment, "God does not give us grace for our imaginations, but for the real trials when they come." Even greater encouragement is to be found in the words of our Lord Jesus, anticipating such events as this coming in to the lives of some of us. He says, "But make up your mind not to worry beforehand how you will defend yourselves. For I will give you words and wisdom that none of your adversaries will be able to resist or contradict" (Luke 21: 14-15).

It is interesting to note that in Jordan in January of 1996, Crown Prince Hassan, King Hussein's brother, and a devout Muslim, sponsored the opening of a Christian Studies Center in Amman, for the purpose of monitoring the treatment of Christians in Muslim countries.

Besides perfecting her facility in the Arabic language during the years in Baraka, God introduced her to the most important person in Aileen's life, other than the Lord Himself. It was here that she met Dr. Eleanor Soltau, thoracic physician on the staff at the hospital. Eleanor, the daughter of a Presbyterian missionary/minister, had been born in Korea, where her parents served as evangelistic missionaries. (Returning to the States because of the Japanese invasion of China in World War II, Eleanor's father, Dr. Soltau, became the beloved pastor of the First Evangelical Church in Memphis, Tennessee.) Eleanor had grown up in Korea while her longtime friend, Ruth Bell, daughter of medical missionaries, Dr. and Mrs. L. Nelson Bell, was growing up in China. They first met at a boarding school for far east missionary children, which was located in Korea. Later these two young ladies attended Wheaton College together, where Ruth met and later married Billy Graham. Eleanor went on to medical school.

Eventually, Aileen and Eleanor realized they had serious theological differences with the hospital leadership in Baraka. That, coupled with the fact that most of the Bedouin tribes were on the east side of the Jordan River, caused them to choose to move nearer to the people they were called to serve. So, in 1965, they decided to begin a work themselves. What an immense undertaking. What a challenge. What courage. Think of it—two women, starting out alone, in an environment hostile to both their sex and their Christian religion. Yet, their miracle of mercy—a completely equipped sixty bed tuberculosis hospital—was accomplished by 1973. "With man, this is impossible, but with God all things are possible" (Matt. 19:26).

As I thought of this unbelievably difficult endeavor, I asked Aileen to tell me how and where it all began. She said, "After our disagreement with Baraka Hospital Administration, I returned with Eleanor to the United States. We wanted to share our new dream for a healing ministry among the Bedouins with our friends and supporters. Naively, we thought that they would all be as happy and enthusiastic as we were about our new vision. But we soon learned otherwise. Two women going into the Arab world, doing things that usually only men did, failed to produce the response we had hoped for. Quite the contrary."

"But one day, when we were visiting in the home of our good friend, Roy Gustafson, he asked us, 'What do you want to do?' In a rather defensive manner, I told him. He listened with interest, and then reached for his Bible, and read to us from Ecclesiastes 11:4-6. 'Whoever watches the wind will not plant; whoever looks at the clouds will not reap.' Then he read, 'Sow your seed in the morning and at evening let not your hands be idle, for you do not know which will succeed, whether this or that; or whether both will do equally well.' Then he closed his Bible and, with a smile, said: 'If you're so convinced that this is what God wants you to do, what are you doing sitting in my living room? Just get up and do it.' So with a few assurances like his and a few encouraging souls in Eleanor's home church in Memphis, we returned to Jordan in 1965."

What gutsy women. Both of them had had tuberculosis themselves. (Aileen twice and Eleanor twice. Eleanor had to drop out of medical school for two years. After practicing medicine for two years, she had to have a lung removed.) So they are both returning to start—what else? A tuberculosis sanitorium. What a call. What obedience. What a vision.

After arriving in Mafraq, Jordan, the first thing they needed, of course, was a building suitable to convert into a hospital. They had only fifty dollars between them, so this constituted a massive problem. They finally found one they thought would work. It was the only stone structure in the whole village of Mafraq. But the owner needed a thousand dollars, the first year's rent, in advance. This was God's work they longed to do, so it was God they went to for help. He immediately provided the first of His many solutions to follow. Just at the right time a check came in the mail. This was a long-forgotten investment which Eleanor had made when practicing medicine in Memphis, Tennessee, many years before. The firm, needing to know how to further invest the money, and having heard nothing from Eleanor, simply closed the account and mailed her the entire proceeds. The size of the check? $1,100.00 End of the first miracle. It was precisely the beautiful and encouraging confirmation they needed from God, and the fulfillment of His promise, "But my God shall supply all your need, according to His riches in glory, by Christ Jesus" (Phil. 4:19).

Six months later they opened the building as a hospital. It had taken them six months just to scrub it squeaky clean enough to use. The initial equipment they employed was partly donated by some doctors in Memphis. They began accepting patients when the hospital had but the barest of necessities.

In the beginning it was a daily challenge to convince the Bedouins to forsake their primitive, superstitious methods of treatment for the modern medical approach, which these professionals knew was the only way to bring healing. What they confronted were such things as the stitching of the stomach with string in order to relieve abdominal pain; burning the external flesh with a red-hot spike in order to drive out the disease; or wearing charms in order to ward off evil spirits. Little by little they earned the trust and respect of the Bedouins, as they saw healing come through the strange, to them, but effective methods of these two loving women. The number of patients began to grow as the word spread through the mysterious "desert telegraph" that here, healing could be found. Because they always prayed with their patients and shared the gospel of Jesus with them, it became known in the desert as the "preaching hospital." On one occasion a member of the royal family of Saudi Arabia bypassed their incredible medical facilities and elected to come to the "preaching hospital" in the North of Jordan. After a stay of several months, she went home completely healed.

They remained in this crowded twenty-one hundred square foot building for eight years. They had accommodations for only sixteen residential patients and several stray cats, which had come for handouts. All the rest of the patients who came had to be treated on an outpatient basis until a bed opened up in the hospital.

About halfway through their eight years in this tiny stone building, they began to realize their desperate need for larger facilities. Typical of their mode of operation, they spoke to their Father in Heaven about their need for increased financial support, and they spoke to their supporters about their vision. We know this to be a fact because my husband led tours to the Middle East in 1968, '69, '70, '77, and '79. Each time the group met with Aileen, she would always share the vision, and inspire us with their work, but you'd have to drag out of her specific monetary, supply and equipment needs that the gifts of the tour members might fill. She told me that, in the beginning, they wanted to make sure that God was in the work, so they went only to Him about money. It was rather like when Jesus first sent His disciples out. He told them to take nothing with them ". . . no purse, bag, or extra sandals" (Luke 10:1-4).

They had to learn to trust Him for everything. But later in their ministry He asked the disciples: "When I sent you without purse, bag, or sandals, did you lack anything?" "Nothing," they said. He said to them, "But now, if you have a purse, take it, and also a bag, and if you don't have a sword, sell your cloak and buy one." Now, He told them to make provision. So, when they felt that God knew they trusted Him alone for their every need, they became more comfortable in making their specific financial needs known to others. I have never met anyone in my whole life who was more sure of the words: "Unless the Lord builds the house, they labor in vain that build it" (Ps. 127:1).

However, even as some funds came in, nagging questions remained unanswered: Who could they afford to get to build the hospital? How could they pay an architect to provide the design? And how would you design a hospital that the Bedouins, who only live in tents, would come to and still feel comfortable, even though cooped up in surroundings they had never before experienced? Questions. Questions. Questions.

Well, let God's miraculous answers unfold before your very eyes.

⇨ ENTER, ANNOOR HOSPITAL.

This is Aileen and Eleanor in front of their first hospital in Mafraq. This was their first prized Volvo, which was stolen by the PLO in the 1966 uprising.

Chapter Three

I Can't Do Much of Anything . . .

One cannot speak of the beginning of Annoor Hospital without telling the heartwarming story of Lester Gates.

He was a recently widowed, successful farmer from Ohio, whose children gave him a trip to the Middle East, wishing to help him through his very difficult time of mourning.

He heard Aileen speak in Jerusalem in 1965 and was so impressed with the work. When he returned to America, he wrote Aileen a letter. In it he said, "*I can't do much of anything*, but I'm sure I could help repair your rented building, and perhaps, build better cupboards than you or Eleanor could." He offered to come for six months, as a self-supporting volunteer. Of course, they leaped at the offer and invited him to come. They quickly discovered that *there wasn't much of anything that this humble servant of God couldn't do.* He was one of those unusual men who, without any formal training, was accomplished in every aspect of construction and maintenance. He not only put the old stone hospital into tiptop shape, but also ended up constructing the new hospital using only local, untrained laborers. He organized, mobilized, and directed this labor with unbelievable efficiency. He never knew more than a few words of Arabic, and the laborers knew little or no English. His primary piece of equipment was one cement mixer, which he donated, and a pickup truck that he brought with him from America when he arrived in 1966.

The six months he promised stretched into twenty-two years. (Another miracle.) All this time he was completely self-supporting. He planted the hundreds of trees on the property—some of which he brought with him, as baggage, when he returned from a brief visit to his family in Ohio. (Their peaches and nectarines are the best in Jordan, according to Aileen.)

He also introduced "drip irrigation" into Jordan long before anyone else was using it. This form of irrigation saves enormous amounts of precious water by avoiding the excessive evaporation associated with sprinkling. To accomplish this task he brought miles of hose upon return from his visits home. He was a man who found great joy in spending his money to further the work of the Lord, both in Mafraq and in other parts of the world. But, let's go back to when he first arrived in Mafraq, and fill in some of the exciting specifics of these beginnings.

Lester had not been there long when he realized, as they did, that their present rented facility was far too small. He kept saying, "Why don't you build?" But, that, of course, brings us back to those "Questions. Questions. Questions." Where would they get the needed money, the land, and the plans?

In those days, foreigners in Jordan were not permitted to own land. But through various friends in the government, who presented a letter to the council of ministers in the capital, Amman, they were granted permission to buy land on which to build a hospital. (This was in spite of the fact that the government knew that they were Christian missionaries. In a Moslem nation this usually is not allowed.) Another miracle.

Eleanor had a friend from her Wheaton College days in America, Bob Van Kampen. Precisely at this time, he *happened* to send her a check for one thousand dollars, with a letter that said: "I'm a business man, and I think it's very poor business for you girls to be paying rent; so why don't you take this money and use it toward buying some land?" With this obvious and encouraging confirmation from God, they began their search for land that would be suitable for a hospital site. Lester, this unique, multi-talented man, began looking over the land outside of Mafraq to choose the area he felt God wanted them to use.

Being a farmer, there were several things that Lester wanted to assure himself about prior to any purchase. First and foremost they needed water, but were beyond the reach of the Mafraq village water supply. But how do you find out what's beneath the desert sands in a place where water is like gold? So Lester carefully selected the dried branch of a scrubby tree that was shaped like a "Y." There were no smaller branches or leaves left on it. Gingerly holding this primitive apparatus with the top of the "Y" in each of his two hands, he began to stomp on the dusty ground, crisscrossing back and forth across the desert. (This little "Y"-shaped branch is variously known as a "dousing rod" or a "witching stick.") As he pounded the earth with his feet marching to and fro, suddenly with no apparent movement on his part, the stick pointed straight down. He marked the spot, continued his marching, and came back to the same place from a different angle. Once again, the stick pointed straight down at the previously made mark. Casually, but with complete confidence, Lester announced: "This is where we will drill and find water" (even though the "experts" assured him there was none there). He also announced that this particular parcel of land would be ideal for the foundation of the hospital, having sensed while parading about that there was subsurface rock under the sand. *Both predictions were absolutely right.* Water was found at that exact spot, and the foundations of the hospital were securely built on solid bedrock. He also preferred the look and feel of the soil for the fulfillment of his agricultural plans. The lush, oasis-like growth on the present hospital compound confirms that he was right again.

Lester was so convinced that his predictions were right that he went back to America, sold his house, and financed the drilling of the well. With this buried treasure they were able to irrigate the trees, orchards, and gardens that were planted while he was building the hospital. And, if you can believe it, for two thousand dollars they were able to buy this God-selected twenty-five acres of desert upon which to build their dream hospital.

Because of the several wars that occurred during this time—the Six-Day war of 1967, and the later, tragic 1970 civil war (instigated by the PLO), plus the Yom Kippur war of 1973—they were often delayed because they couldn't get building materials and the general supplies needed for construction. The most appalling reason for delay was the fact that Lester was brutally beaten, and then expelled from the country. The expulsion came as result of false complaints made by the Iraqi army. (The Iraqis had positioned themselves in Mafraq directly after the Six Day War of 1967.) Five months after his expulsion he was given permission to return, having been completely exonerated. Many advised them not to proceed because of the uncertainty of the times. Due to the ongoing turmoil in the entire Middle East, no construction of any kind was recommended. But, as God enabled them, they continued to build, and when they couldn't, Lester planted trees. So, by the time the hospital was ready for occupancy, in 1973, they had an orchard of several thousand olive and other fruit trees. They were also given eight thousand small pine trees by the minister of agriculture. As the hospital is in a very sandy desert, Lester used these pine trees to grow a windbreak fence all around the property.

Lester Gates was also an amazing man when it came to managing money. He could really stretch a dollar. Again, although he was not a trained contractor, he demonstrated that he was a highly intelligent and talented builder. He constructed that entire sixty-bed hospital for seventy thousand dollars. It was made with hand-cut local sandstone, which is not only very beautiful, but also represents the best construction in that culture. The hospital surrounds open courtyards so the Bedouin patients who are used to tent dwellings in the open desert don't feel closed in.

And, what about the question of an appropriate architect to design the hospital? Well, God provided them with a young man from California, Raymond Luley. He was a recent college graduate who needed practice in drawing up plans for a hospital. And, my, did he practice professionally. He did his due diligence in educating himself to the traditions of Arabic design by writing to several architects that worked in Iran. From them he learned much about the cultural concepts which were acceptable for a hospital in a Muslim country. That, plus Aileen's input, made him aware of the danger of Bedouins fearing the idea of being "locked in." For most of them their hospital visit was the first time they had ever slept in anything other than a tent. For this reason, Luley's design included the outside walls being serrated so that each patient has his or her own large window. Patients can *see* outside even when they can't *be* outside. Raymond Luley, glad for the experience, generously gave all his services and the detailed plans, which Lester so faithfully followed.

The hospital was built slowly. Lester was always happy to have volunteer workers from America, even though few of them had any experience in construction work. Most of them came for a summer, although some stayed longer. They were usually university students who were ready to spend their vacation time in the scalding summer heat, amidst the dust and flies that are a part of desert life. Aileen said, "They have been a great help to us, and have kept us young. Even though it was frustrating at times, it's great to see the way God has worked in the lives of many of these young people. Three of them are now on the board of directors of the Mafraq Sanitorium Association: David Schultz, Sally (Gilman) Dove, and Franklin Graham, now chairman of the hospital board, president of Samaritan's Purse, and heir-apparent to his father's world wide ministry. Others have gone into Christian work: Bill Bell is pastor of a large church in America; Bill Cristobel is a missionary pilot in New Guinea; and Mark Taylor is president of Tyndale House Publishing, one of the largest Christian publishing houses in the world."

Aileen was also quick to say: "It wasn't that we had such a profound impact on these young people, but rather what God was doing in the lives of these volunteer workers. Because there were no entertainment diversions in Mafraq to distract them, they had plenty of time to listen to God and learn to obey him. Lester worked them so hard they were too exhausted to do anything at the end of the day except collapse in bed. So we were thrilled to see how God has blessed and used them. The absence of funds made their contribution of labor very important."

"Speaking of money," Aileen said: "In the beginning, as previously mentioned, one of the unusual sources of funding came from the innumerable tours led by Roy Gustafson and others, sponsored by the Billy Graham Association. After either I, or Eleanor, spoke to the tour group, Roy would make known specific needs we currently had at the hospital. Then individual members of the group would volunteer to meet that need with a contribution. Also, the Billy Graham Association contributed liberally to the work. Lester Gates, himself, was the next largest donor.

When Franklin Graham and David Schultz returned from their first summer here, in the late 1960s, they went on deputation for us and raised a great deal of money. Tyndale House Publishers matched their total, mainly because Mark Taylor had been here during that same summer. Sally Gilman Dove, on her return to the States, raised enough money for us to buy a red station wagon. We still get some support from those individuals who heard of the hospital while on those tours." There have been many other selfless individual gifts; and after all these years of demonstrated effectiveness in healing body and soul, additional churches and organizations have written the hospital into their annual missionary budgets.

In later years, as they became more organized, a board of directors was appointed. When Franklin Graham became president of Samaritan's Purse, he made available to the hospital the logistical resources of that organization as well as considerable financial assistance. They not only mail out the hospital's quarterly newsletter, from their headquarters in Boone, North Carolina, but they also issue tax-deductible receipts to donors. The Annoor Hospital Newsletter contains a straightforward account of just the news of the hospital, including a letter from Aileen. Appeals for funds for the hospital are usually found in the Samaritan's Purse publications.

God continues to mysteriously move on the hearts of individuals and churches. Although the hospital often falls short of their annual financial needs, at "just the right time" God sends the appropriate, unexpected gifts to balance the books. It is important to note that they never built or planted beyond their means. Borrowing money never seemed to be in their thoughts.

The nurses' home wasn't finished until fifteen years after the completion of the hospital. Even though it is half the size of the hospital, it cost twice as much money to construct. (Note: Lester Gates did not build the nurses' home.) This building is the residence of the nurses, single missionary women, and female domestic staff.

The hospital now serves over 150,000 wandering Bedouin and twenty thousand people living in Mafraq. It has been doing this for nearly three decades.

Lester Gates worked with them those twenty-two years, selflessly, unsung, without any recognition. He didn't want it, and he never sought it.

He suffered a severe heart attack during a Christmas visit with his family and had four-way bypass surgery. He was back in Jordan in early March. Aileen said, "His daughter, Mrs. Jeri Severt, called us from Ohio and asked us to try to make Lester take things a little slower than his usual pace. Eleanor spoke to him firmly, as a physician, exhorting him to rest after lunch and to quit working early in the afternoon. Lester just smiled and said nothing. The next morning, when I went to breakfast at 6:30 A.M., I noticed him plowing on the tractor. He stayed there until it was too dark for him to see anymore. So much for our concern and exhortation." Then, as she allowed her thoughts to go back to 1966, with tears in her eyes, she said, "Lester was fifty-six when he arrived in Mafraq. He lived in a mud house in the town. One night we had an unusually heavy rain. The next morning found him sleeping on the street because the heavy rain had caused the wall of his bedroom to collapse. Yet, he never complained. People who worked with him as laborers thirty years ago will still stop me on the street today and remind me of the respect and affection they had for him." Then she added, "He was a generous, humble man, with the heart of a servant, whose reward is great in heaven."

He left Jordan in 1988 and returned to his daughter's home because of ill health. He died in November of 1994. What an inspiring example he is of what God can do through any person who sincerely seeks to please Him and doesn't care who gets the credit. He was just a tourist who made himself available to God for whatever He had in mind for his future. He could not have known how great were the Lord's plans for him as he obeyed. Consider the unpretentious greatness of this unassuming, unheralded man who introduced himself to Aileen with these words:

➪ "I CAN'T DO MUCH OF ANYTHING . . ."

(left to right) Eleanor, Lester, Franklin Graham, and Aileen

Chapter Four

God's Gift of People for the Work

In addition to Lester Gates, the Lord brought some wonderful Jordanian people in to share the ministry with Aileen and Eleanor.

In the beginning, it was just Nasri Khoury and his wife, Manahi Hadad. Nasri is the son of a Greek Orthodox priest, from Beit Sahour (which is the Shepherd's Fields, near Bethlehem). Manahi is from a well-known family in Jordan. In 1962, they were both student nurses in the Baraka Hospital, in Bethlehem, when Aileen and Eleanor were there. When they crossed the river and went to Mafraq, Jordan, Nasri and Manahi joined them as part of the original team. Their large family prevented Manahi from being actively involved in the nursing aspect of the ministry until their children were grown.

From the very beginning until now, Nasri has been their most faithful and fruitful male evangelist. Aileen said, "Nasri has proven to be a man full of compassion, with a great love for the Bedouin people. They, in turn, respond to that love, and have complete confidence in him." She then added, nostalgically, "I can remember, in one of the wars, when Mafraq was under attack, I looked out and saw six women—all clinging to him because they were so afraid—asking for his protection and help during the bombing. This was an amazing sight because, in the Bedouin culture, women do not touch men. His great love for the patients opens many doors for them to hear the gospel." Continuing on with great affection and appreciation for this servant of Christ, Aileen said, "I've seen men admitted to this hospital so ill that they couldn't even care for their own personal needs. Nasri nurses them as if they were his own infant children. And, he does it with a tenderness that *always preserves their dignity*. Because of this they will, sufficiently recovered, begin to voluntarily come to our meetings every night. We've then found them much more ready to hear the Good News, due to the fact that this Arab brother has shown them such authentic 'love-of-Christ-in-action.' "

It is to Nasri that Aileen looks for help in hanging on to the original vision with which she and Eleanor began and to fight any temptation that others might have to turn away from this God-given goal. (In some cases, second generation workers fail to see the Bedouins as the wonderful people they are . . . there is always such a pull to be with people of more sophistication, greater cleanliness, and education . . . people who have so many other ways to hear the Good News than do these children of Ishmael.) Nasri sees eye-to-eye and heart-to-heart with them. He is truly one of God's greatest gifts to them for the work, and he's been steadfastly at it for over thirty-three years, leaving a trail of people behind him who reflect the love of Jesus—a love that first came to them through Nasri's touch of healing.

He has also been a tremendous help as a liaison between the hospital and the government administration. "Being an Arab," Aileen said, "he knows how to handle the officials. He has been used of God in so many difficult situations, helping us to find solutions that we, as foreigners, could never find. But, mainly, it's his faithfulness, loyalty, and his love for the Bedouins that have made him such an indispensable part of the staff and work at the Mafraq Sanitorium."

They have always trained their own Jordanian nurses who have come, for the most part, from the villages nearby. This presents a tremendous challenge to them in many areas. It's very different from training nurses in the West. Most of these girls, before they come to them, have never slept in a bed. So they don't understand why they should make patients' beds everyday. This, then, makes their training quite difficult and frustrating. But, Aileen says, "In the end it makes it so worthwhile to see these young men and women taking on the responsibility of giving patients first class care. Our hospital, compared to the West, is very basic. I guess you might even call it primitive. And, yet, we have a reputation in Jordan, especially, of being one of the places where patients get excellent care." (And it's not easy to dispense this good care to patients who don't easily accept treatment, or take their prescribed drugs, or even stay in their beds. But I can attest to this, because I've seen it with my own eyes: *they know they're loved*).

"And, of course, while these dear Jordanians are with us," Aileen said, "we have the opportunity of leading them to Jesus Christ. Some of them have become real partners in the ministry. They have seen their nursing not just as a means of having an education, or producing a livelihood, but as a means of being able to serve God as they care for the patients." She went on to say, "It's heartwarming to see how deeply attached they get to the patients. It's not uncommon to see the Jordanian student and graduate nurses weeping as some of our babies are discharged. They get so emotionally involved with them—just as we do—that they hate to give them up. These Jordanian students come to us ignorant and uneducated, yet leave us, so often, as men and women of commendable stature. This is especially true for the girls who are able to return home to be married, with the new ability to take care of their own babies and families in a much more efficient and health-giving manner."

Before leaving the subject of the challenge and frustrating aspects sometimes involved in attempting to train the Jordanian worker, I must interject an amusing anecdote. Aileen was forced to call on her great sense of humor for this one. She said, "This is a really different culture and we're continually needing to adjust and adapt to it. Most of our garden labor around the hospital is done by Jordanian men. They come to us knowing nothing about our 'crazy Western ways.' They are always anxious to please us, but often fall quite short of it. I remember, once, we had a simple young man working in the garden who watched me every day as I checked the fruit trees for ripe fruit. We had a large crop of peaches which I examined early every morning. When I found a tree with ripe fruit, I would 'flag it' with a piece of white bandage. Then Ratib (the young laborer) would pick the ripe peaches on that tree.

"One day, I went into the kitchen in the afternoon, and I found several boxes of peaches that were so green and so hard they couldn't be used for anything—not even jam. So I called Ratib in and said, 'What's the story on these peaches? Why did you pick the green ones?' He said, 'I did just what you did. I tied a piece of bandage on the tree and then went and picked them.' He hadn't quite related the white bandage to the ripened peaches. Obviously he had tried to please me and make me happy, but there was nothing we could do but have him bury the green peaches. Having watched what I did, he somehow associated the white bandage on the tree as producing the ripened peaches, rather than seeing already ripened peaches and marking the tree with the bandage."

It takes a lot of patience, know-how, and a good sense of humor to successfully train the Jordanian workers, but most of all it takes a heart full of love. Aileen possesses an abundance of that. Fiercely protective of both the Bedouins and the Jordanians, she will be certain to assure one and all that, once trained, these people are most productive and faithful workers. She is endearingly defensive about their culture where their practices might raise some questions. She will then go into great detail to give you the rationale for the customs, lauding all of their commendable attributes. She exemplifies Proverbs 10:12 in her attitude toward the people to whom she has dedicated her life; "Love covers over all wrongs."

In considering God's gift of people for the work, a person who stands out because of her unique and invaluable contribution is Her Royal Highness Shareefih Zein Bint Nasser—Princess Zein—cousin of King Hussein of Jordan. Aileen and the princess met in a most amazing and interesting way.

Over ten years ago, Princess Zein was speaking at one of the meetings of the Ministries of Social Development in Amman, the capital city. Among the things of which she spoke was her observation that nothing was being done for the Bedouin. Whereupon someone stood up and stated very clearly, "Oh, yes there is. There is a place in Mafraq where a great work is being done." The response of the princess was, "Then, I'd like to see it." Her first attempt was amazingly, and amusingly, obstructed by one of the hospital's own employees.

Princess Zein arrived at the Annoor Sanitorium unexpected, unannounced, and unrecognized. When the princess asked to tour the hospital and see the work, one of the nurses said to her, very kindly, "I'm sorry, but we don't allow visitors during the patients' rest hour." However, the nurse did run quickly and get a little girl named Noorah, whom Aileen had raised from an infant, to show the kind and patient visitor. Demonstrating her own humility, the princess left without protest and without identifying herself. Sometime later she phoned back and spoke to Aileen, identifying herself, and then simply saying, "I tried to get in but couldn't because the patients were resting." Needless to say, Aileen apologizing for what had happened felt chagrin and embarrassment. Immediately, the princess defended the nurse, saying, "Rules must be followed by everyone. That's why you have them." However, you can be sure that when the princess arrived the next time she had no trouble getting in, and, indeed, received a royal welcome. From the first visit until now, she never visits the hospital without bringing toys for the sick children, plus an assortment of other items to help the work.

This was the beginning of a wonderful relationship that has only deepened through the years. All of us have fanciful dreams about what a real live princess's life would be like. She, like all the members of the royal family, is deeply involved in hard work on behalf of the people of Jordan. Hardly an event takes place, even a minor function, without at least one of the members of the royal family present to celebrate with the participants and give encouragement to those who have caused the progress. The princess has made herself available to the work of Annoor Hospital over the years, serving alongside Aileen and Eleanor, often on occasions of trauma out in the wilds of the desert, selflessly giving herself to help her beloved Bedouins. These shared events have brought them very close in a growing friendship of mutual respect and affection. Aileen shares: "I have learned so much about Bedouin culture by accompanying Princess Zein, as we have visited tribes in the desert."

The princess is relatively young, very attractive, well educated at a university in the United States, and with all of the sophistication that one would expect of a person born to royalty. She is a direct descendant of the Prophet Mohammed. But when she treks into the desert with Aileen to help the Bedouin, she is completely Bedouin in dress, culture, and behavior. The two of them together could be taken for Bedouin women. Though the tribes-people know who has come to help them, she assumes no airs of royalty, and pitches in to do whatever is called for by the needs around them: handing out blankets, food, clothing, shoes, or assisting in the administration of medicines along with the "Doctorahs." When the primitive food of the desert is served, the princess is sitting on the ground with Aileen and the rest, eating whatever is offered.

In explaining their desert adventures, Aileen said, "Sometimes we've worked together in times of severe crisis. Several years ago Jordan was hit by an unusually severe snow storm. Six feet of snow fell in the southern part of Jordan. The Bedouins have rarely ever seen that kind of snow in their entire lifetime, so they were not prepared for the devastating impact of such an event. As soon as Princess Zein heard of their plight, she asked me to go with her to see if we could help. When we arrived, we found that some of the tents had collapsed under the weight of the snow, killing all the sheep and the goats which had been brought into the tents for warmth and protection. The Bedouins had been able to escape from under the tents, but the animals couldn't. The snow reached as high as their thighs, and the poor people were standing, barefooted, in the snow. It was a terrifying situation in the remote regions of the desert, and so far away from any kind of help. Dead animals, chickens, and birds were scattered everywhere in the snow. People who had survived were standing around, confused and shivering outside what used to be their homes. We were overwhelmed with the enormity of the tragedy. Through the good offices of Princess Zein, Jordanian Army forces were put at our disposal. Their enormous trucks could make it through the deep snow drifts where ordinary transports couldn't have succeeded." As they bounced along in the desert, where no roads existed, Aileen turned to Eleanor and said: "If we lived another lifetime we wouldn't be able to reach the people hidden this far out, in these remote regions." Accompanied by the princess, they found encampment after encampment of Bedouins in utter chaos. "For days Zein, Eleanor, and I reached out to people most affected by the storm. We distributed clothes, blankets, and basic food supplies. Princess Zein worked tirelessly among the people from dawn until dusk. I saw her crying several times through grief and frustration—frustration, because she couldn't replace their lost flocks and grief as she saw the distress of the people we came to help. She is truly a woman of substance—a woman of great compassion. 'She stretched out her hands to the poor; yea, she reached forth her hands to the needy' "(Prov. 31:20).

In one of the first encampments where they stopped to help, a woman came rushing up to Aileen and said: "Don't you remember me?" Aileen explained, "She'd been in our Mafraq hospital ten years before. She'd had to stay there several months for her treatment. We'd lost contact with her after she'd recovered, as they'd travelled many miles away. (As a matter of fact, this snow storm occurred nearer to Ras A Naqab, where the clinic was now set in place, 185 miles away from Mafraq.) I asked her what she had remembered from her time with us. Amazingly, she sang many of the Christian hymns she'd learned. Then she shared her very simple but very firm faith. She still had complete assurance that her sins had been forgiven, and that she was, indeed, a child of God. She had remembered that redeeming message of Jesus Christ that she had heard while being treated for tuberculosis, in our Annoor Hospital in Mafraq—so many years ago and so far away."

After hearing this testimony, Aileen and Eleanor exchanged a knowing glance—remembering how they had just said, "We'll never be able to reach people this far out in the desert." Here was the evidence that God had devised a plan whereby He had already—through them—placed one of His chosen in the midst of the tribe.

Further confirmation of God's wondrous ways of doing things met them at the next encampment they visited. This time it was a man who rushed up to them, jubilantly, with the very same question: "Don't you remember me. I slept in your hospital." (This Bedouin term makes it sound like an overnight stay. What he meant was that he had slept in that hospital for several months while his tuberculosis was being healed.) When Aileen asked this tribesman the same question she'd put to the woman in the previous encampment, he also responded with a very clear and current statement of his faith in Christ's redeeming work in his life. He said he was sure of his forgiveness, and sure of Heaven, because of what his Risen Saviour had done and was continuing to do for him.

Consider the keeping power of God's Holy Spirit in these individuals. Recognizing the absence of the usual means of grace—daily Bible study and the encouragement of other believers—it is remarkable. It illustrates so beautifully Christ's promises: "I will never leave you nor forsake you . . . ," and "Lo, I Am with you always, even unto the ends of the earth" (Heb. 13:5b, Matt. 28:20b). Once again, Aileen and Eleanor rejoiced together at the realization that God was way far ahead of them in His strategy to save His people anywhere.

"Even in times of extreme suffering and stress, the Bedouin people showed their amazing resilience: They were eager to show their ever-present hospitality, and did their utmost to make fires out of wet wood, so they could offer that traditional cup of sweet tea, even as we were there to help them." Aileen went on, "We tried hard, very hard, to match clothes with the sizes of the children. One little girl, about 9-years-old, came to the truck where I was distributing clothes. She said, 'My name is Falaahah, and I want a red coat and red boots.' We had some used red coats and red boots, but nothing in her size. I tried to convince her that she would look great in new black boots and a yellow coat that would fit her. No success. She hobbled off in too-small red boots, and a much too-big red coat. She knew what she wanted and wouldn't settle for anything else." One can conclude that "girls will be girls" wherever they live.

It is their mutual love and respect for the Bedouin people that has brought Princess Zein and Aileen into an ever deepening friendship through the years.

Both Princess Zein and her cousin, King Hussein, have tremendous pride in their heritage. As previously mentioned, both are direct descendants of Mohammed, and they are both from the Heshamite tribe of Bedouins. King Hussein's grandfather, King Abdullah, continued to keep his grandson in close touch with his heritage. He had a traditional Bedouin tent at a remote place on the palace grounds, and once or twice a year the king would go to live in the tent even as his forbears had for thousands of years. On occasion he would take his grandson, Hussein, with him to remind him of his roots. King Hussein continues the practice to this very day.

Princess Zein also makes sure that her children respect and remember their Bedouin heritage. When they were younger, she brought them to the Annoor Hospital to visit the sick children, and to share with them some of their own toys as gifts. Although her son, Layth, is off at college now, the princess will often bring her daughter, Zwein, along to visit the tents in the desert. On occasion Zwein has spent part of her vacation in the tents, while others from her school might have been in Paris, or at the Riviera. When "show and tell" time comes during the school year, Zwein may well share her desert experience of chasing mice from the tents.

Because of the special relationship that exists between Aileen and the princess—a Christian missionary and a Muslim Princess—a very interesting question was asked by the host of the Australian version of the "Sixty Minutes" television program. The work of the Annoor Hospital was the subject of the program, and he inquired of the princess, "How can it be that you, a Muslim, have such a close and helpful friendship with a person who is doing Christian missionary work in your country?" The princess responded, "When any others show the kind of love, compassion, and healing mercy to my people that she has through this ministry, then I will be happy to assist them as well."

On that last evening of our visit to Jordan, when we were the guests of the princess for dinner, it was beautiful to observe the bond of genuine friendship that exists between them. They are truly "laborers together with God. They are God's field, His building" (1 Cor. 3:9).

From the original cadre of stalwarts who brought this remarkable ministry to pass in the desert, it is heartwarming to see how He's continued to gather together people from all walks of life—doctors, nurses, farmers, evangelists, gardeners, kitchen help, yes, even princesses—"God's lovely gift of people for the work."

Nasri Khoury and wife, Menahi, in front of their home, built by Lester Gates

"Friends in the Cause of Mercy" — (near the Dead Sea) Princess Zein, a direct descentdant of Mohammed, and Aileen Coleman, Christian missionary nurse

Aileen and the Princess doing relief work in the aftermath of a terrible snow storm

Chapter Five

Adjusting and Trusting

There is a great culture shock just between the Western world and the modern part of the Muslim world. There is an even more profound culture shock when one's call is to the Bedouins in the desert. Their lifestyle goes way back to the days of Abraham who was the first nomadic Bedouin.

When Aileen and Eleanor first went to Mafraq, their living quarters were very crowded and extremely primitive. They fought and continue to fight, regular dust storms, having to tolerate that devastating condition for at least seven months of the year. (Not to mention the intense heat and dryness that accompanies this climate.)

In the beginning they shared a bedroom, because there was no alternative, and they took turns sleeping in the hospital with the patients. After they moved into the new hospital they lived in very small rooms close to the patients. It was, and is, always cold in the winter because they choose to keep it that way to accommodate the Bedouin patients, who, in the winter have very little heat in their tents. They wanted the hospital to be like the tents, so that when the patients returned to their tents, they would not have become accustomed to a level of heat they could no longer maintain. They also feared that by keeping them too warm they might endanger the patients with the possibility of pneumonia upon their return to their homes. This meant that they had to learn to wear layers of clothing, like the Bedouin, in order to keep warm even when they're in the hospital. Since 1988, they have lived in a more comfortable nurses' residence with a little more space, and, though they still battle those abominable dust storms, Aileen says they have just chosen not to see the dust anymore. (Which makes her my most favorite house guest.)

Aileen is quick to admit that they're not threatened by wild animals, or a lot of miserable things their missionary friends encounter in other parts of the world. But the one thing they are plagued with—that they see the most and like the least—are the ubiquitous rats that are a constant part of their lives. Their food (and clothing) all have to be stored in metal containers, because the rats will chew through boxes and plastic, even the hardiest Tupperware. I have witnessed the remains of ruined luggage with my own eyes. They are irrepressible. Which brings me to this horrendous Hitchcockian tale, that I suggest you read in the daytime.

They had a community cat they called "Toots." She had a rather strange ritual whereby she would visit each one of them at night. She'd make the rounds—wander into a room, sleep for a while in one bed, then depart, and go to the next room. One night, Aileen remembers waking up and feeling the cat on her neck, which was nothing unusual. So she said, "Hi Toots," and began stroking her hair and carrying on the sweetest, softest, cat-conversation she could manage at that hour of the night. After she had been petting her for some time, a light suddenly went on in her head. "Toots has long hair and this cat has short hair." So on went the other light!! To her heart-stopping-horror, she saw that she had been sharing that intimate interlude with a huge rat, who'd snuggled into her neck. She said the rat didn't seem to be at all concerned or disturbed when she switched the light on. Moreover, he was in no particular hurry. He just strolled off her bed. Some of her nurse friends later asked, "Did you scream?" To which she responded: "There was no point in screaming because nobody could do anything about it." (I feel she might have at least succeeded in deafening the rat. I know that I would have given a go at splitting his ear drums—that is, if I hadn't passed out first.) The rat eventually ambled away, probably to join the other rats that frequent their place at night. This has to be every woman's worst-case-scenario. I would probably still be in recovery. (But that's neither here nor there—more accurately, that's probably one of the many reasons why I'm here and not there.) But, Aileen has an amazing capacity to adjust to such conditions.

In the early days, their patients used to arrive by camel. Now they usually come by pickup trucks; though many still have to come by camel or donkey for their journey to the hospital. It was not an uncommon sight to see camels tied up at the front gate as patients were being treated. The camel is not Aileen's favorite animal. She says they are mean animals, and they'll bite you simply because you're there, not because you have provoked them, or that they have any reason to dislike you. However, when necessary, she will ride them in order to get to where she wants to go.

Having lived with the Bedouin people for over two thirds of her life, the deep love she has for them includes a tremendous amount of respect. She's found them to be tough, but with a great deal of gentleness beneath the tough exterior. She's found them to be uncomplaining, though their life-style is very difficult. They just consider their lot in life to be Allah's will, accept it, and get on with life. All the while they remain basically cheerful. The average life span for a man is fifty years. It is much shorter for a woman.

They are very gracious people. She has never seen hospitality that equals that of the Bedouin people—anywhere. When you arrive at their tents, on the hottest days, they will immediately offer you water—that ever so precious commodity—to wash your feet and hands. When you've come across the desert, this is most refreshing and appreciated. Then you're given the very best they have. Often its very little, but you know that it is something they are depriving themselves or their children of, so that you, as their guest, will have the best they can offer.

As soon as you enter the tent, you're given the traditional sip of bitter, strong Bedouin coffee, followed by sweet, sweet tea. If your business is brief, you get the traditional coffee again, just before you leave. Aileen says she's learned a lot about giving and a lot about receiving as she has lived and worked with these amazing desert dwellers.

One particular experience of "receiving" will always remain close to her heart: "While out visiting the tents," Aileen said, "Eleanor and I entered the dwelling of a mother with five children. She surprised us with a very warm and loving welcome. We had forgotten her, but she remembered us. She had been a patient in the hospital before her marriage, about fifteen years ago. I don't remember ever seeing such poverty. Their tent was in ribbons, and the family lived on a dirt floor—with just a few quilts for furniture. It seemed to us that there was no food around.

"You can imagine how we felt when our former patient gave each of us an egg as a gift. We did try, at first, to refuse it; but she said, 'You told me about Jesus Christ, and He has been with me ever since I repented and accepted Him. You must accept this egg, for I have no other way of giving a gift to Him who loved me and died for me.' "

What an example. Oh, that there were such a heart in us, as we give our tithes and offerings as unto God usually from our abundance, not from our want as did this precious, Bedouin believer. ". . . but she, out of her poverty, put in everything, all she had to live on . . ."(Mark 12:42-44).

Early on in their ministry, they decided they would adapt to the Bedouin culture at every point that did not conflict with the Word of God. Therefore, when they went ministering in the desert, they dressed as the Bedouin women dress. (When she wears their garb, it's hard to distinguish her from the other Bedouin women, except for her height.) When darkness finds them too far from the hospital to make it back, they'll often sleep on the dirt floor of the tent, with the Bedouin women. (There is a rug type curtain which is hung to separate the men from the women.)

The Bedouins don't seem to be unduly worried about their poverty but rather resigned to it perhaps because they've known nothing else. In the spring, when there are lambs and kids from their struggling flocks, they will have lamb and goat meat. They also have cheese and yogurt made from the goat and sheep milk. But, later in the summer, after the grass has died and the desert is back to its usual state, their diet consists of just bread, albeit delicious bread! It is made of whole wheat flour they often grind on the spot and serve with that sweet, sweet tea. It's amazing how well they survive on bread and tea.

Their tents are made of goat's hair that has been spun and woven by the women into strips that are about a yard wide. Then they are sewn together. They make long, low, black tents, in which a whole family and sometimes an extended family lives. (I've even seen a miniature tent made to house a dog.) Most live on a dirt floor, but some of them have rugs to cover the dirt. These Bedouin rugs are made from that same goat's hair and sheep's wool—again, woven by the women. The rugs are dyed with a substance made from either roots or ground-up leaves. They are beautiful dyes—the traditional colors of red, maroon, dark green, beige, cream, brown, and black.

One of the things Aileen particularly admires about them is that the family is very close-knit and supportive of one another. She's impressed with the deep respect that the children have for their elders and that the adults have for their parents. The elderly, in the Bedouin world, are cared for by their families with love and consideration. (She would like to see more of this in the Western world.)

Aileen said, "When the desert Bedouin look inside our western style dwellings, crammed with all our creature comforts, they not only don't envy us, they're likely to respond in bewilderment, 'How can you live with all this stuff?' "

Although according to the Muslim religion, a man can have more than one wife at any given time, there aren't many who have had more than two. They usually can't afford it, and human nature there is about the same as anywhere. Two wives in one tent cause problems. It often leads to jealousies and friction in the home. Moreover, it creates a lot of ill feeling, especially among the children of the two wives. (Occasionally you'll find two wives who've decided to become friends. They can, at times, develop quite a good relationship, helping each other, taking care of each other's children, and, generally, living like sisters, with the same husband.) The Muslim men really love their little girls, spoiling them atrociously at least until they are thirteen and eligible for marriage. (This practice of very early marriage is now being discouraged by the government.)

It is interesting that the dowry price is agreed upon between the girl's father and the family of the groom. The money paid for her hand is supposed to be used to buy the basic needs for the new tent i.e., floor coverings, sleeping pads, and bed covers. The price is regulated by the social standing of the families making the agreement. (Of course, a girl being married for the first time demands a higher price than one who has already been married.) Up to about twenty years ago, camels were often used as payment for a bride. Most marriages are arranged within the tribe. Islam is a classless religion, but in the Bedouin world, there are some tribes known as the "Shurafah Tribes," which means they are the upper class.

Even though the Bedouin people are very poor, they're extremely generous and conscientious. The hospital charges a very nominal fee for hospital care. Seven dollars per month covers everything—hospitalization, medication, examinations, and treatments. But sometimes the patients don't even have this small amount to pay when they are released.

The hospital doesn't maintain extended accounts or records, so no one is ever dunned for nonpayment. Occasionally, years later, someone will come and pay maybe two dollars against their bill for the time spent in the hospital. Aileen finds them to be a great people with a noble sense of responsibility. They never accept a favor without feeling they are duty-bound to return a similar, or greater, favor.

As stated, Aileen and Eleanor purposed from the beginning to adapt to the Middle Eastern culture in every way possible that did not conflict with the Word of God. Well, the day arrived when this decision to adapt to Muslim culture was put to a most severe test.

In their earliest days at Sharjah, they'd helped a woman who had a sterility problem to have a son. She was the much loved wife of one of the tribal elders—a very important sheik. So, in gratitude, the woman invited them to a great banquet she had prepared in Aileen's honor. (It was, of course, just for ladies, as they don't have mixed social gatherings in the Muslim world.) As she was sitting on the floor with several other missionaries with whom she worked, and some Arab ladies of the upper class, an unbelievable feast was brought in. They entered with a huge tray—at least six feet in diameter—completely covered with food. The first layer was rice; the next identifiable item was a small, whole camel, covering most of the rice. The camel was immediately removed and taken out to feed the poor people. (Aileen says she's eaten camel since then, and it's not too bad.) Inside the roasted camel was a roasted whole sheep. Inside the sheep was a roasted desert bird, rather like a turkey. Inside the turkey was a boiled egg (probably having something to do with a sign of fertility).

They sat on the floor, Bedouin style, feeding themselves only with the right hand. The hostess did not eat with them, but only served them. She tore off the choice pieces of meat from the carcass and gave them to each person. All was going well until Aileen noticed that the hostess began to crack open the skull of the sheep. (Having been fed brains by her own mother, as a child, she thought, "Oh, she's going to feed me the brains." She had never liked them, but, out of obedience to her mother, had managed to get them down.) But this is not what the hostess pulled out of the skull. It was one of the sheep's eyes! With that everyone at the party stopped eating and looked to see who was the honoree—the chosen one—who would receive the eye. She did not know, until that very moment, that she was the "Privileged Person." Her heart sank and her mouth began to water. In desperation, she whispered in English to the missionary lady sitting next to her, "What do I do with it?" She answered, "Why you eat it, of course." Heart pounding, she recalled having seen the inside of a human eye during an operation at the nurses training school, and she thought, " 'I simply cannot bite this. I will surely gag if I try to chew it.' And so I decided the only thing to do was to swallow it whole. It wasn't a big sheep, and I was thankful for that." Bravely reaching out, she took the dreaded eyeball, popped it in her mouth and swallowed it in one gigantic gulp. It seemed bigger within the mouth than it had been before. Reluctantly, it slid down. Her eyes then began to water profusely. There seemed to be some question as to whether it would stay down. Some of the tears began running down her cheeks. "I looked at the Arab ladies," she said, "to see what their reaction was. To my amazement, they seemed quite impressed. Then I heard one of them say to another, 'Look, she is so overcome by the honor of having the eye presented to her, that she has been brought to tears.' "

In remembering this early test, Aileen said, "I was so grateful to God, not only that I managed to get the eyeball down . . . not only that I hadn't thrown up all the rest of my food . . . but also that they actually considered my tears expressions of gratitude for the honor of it all."

And this is the rest of the story. As soon as she arrived back at the hospital in Sharjah, she arranged for one of the workers to buy her a sheep's head. Why? So she could cook the eyes and force herself to eat them, should such an honor ever come her way again. That's dedication beyond the call of reasonable duty. But it was a practice that paid off. Many times since then she has been called on to repeat the performance. It has become so commonplace to her that she no longer even thinks about the possibility of gagging. What a woman. That's what you call true adjusting and trusting.

Although the Bedouin people are most gracious, and insist upon returning favors, and although this includes not only their guests, but also foreigners and those of other tribes, it takes a long time for them to fully accept anyone outside of their own tribe. But, once you have a loyal Bedouin friend who fully trusts you, then you can rely on that loyalty for a lifetime. Their loyalty is to a *person,* not to a *cause.* Once you have their friendship, you know you can depend on it forever.

From the beginning the Bedouin people were always gracious to Aileen and Eleanor. But it was not until the Civil War of 1970 that they began to experience the fuller trust and acceptance for which their hearts had longed. On several previous occasions of political or military unrest in the Middle East, both the Australian and American Embassies had strongly advised their departure from Jordan. But, because they desired to stay and care for their patients, they told the ambassadors, "We're not going anywhere. Why should we get out the moment something goes wrong? Are our hides worth more than any one of these poor Bedouins lying here in these wards? They're not going to be sent out of Jordan, so leaving is the last thing on our agenda."*

During the Six-Day War of 1967, Aileen and Eleanor had actually gone to the military and volunteered to assist in the Medical Corps. Floored by the offer, the military thanked them and told them they would be held in reserve, should they be needed. So, when all others evacuated to safety, they remained with their beloved Bedouin in Jordan. Aileen said that they were always aware, daily, of the great peace God gives, even in the midst of flying bullets and conflict. And He gave them His own special protection as they remained in the midst of it all and completely identified with the people. The fact that they stood with the ones they had come to minister to, not only in times of peace, but also in the times of conflict, crisis, and difficulty, did not go unnoticed. It was their God who enabled them to take such a courageous stand, but from a human standpoint, what a great example of adjusting and trusting this was.

It was during the Civil War in 1970 that they lost their cars and some of their equipment. And when some of the staff were badly mistreated and roughed up by the P.L.O. (the forces opposing His Majesty, King Hussein), the Bedouin men made Aileen and Eleanor "Blood Brothers." They did it in the traditional custom, piercing the skin of each party and blending the blood. Making themselves "Blood Brothers" with two females, who were also Christians was simply unheard of when you consider their Muslim culture. This was that tribe's announcement that anyone who showed enmity to these two women automatically declared their enmity to their entire tribe, in perpetuity. Since then, whenever conflict has broken out, several of the tribe will show up with their ancient firearms and take up watch around the hospital compound. They're like a warning red flag to any who would harm them.

---

*Direct quote from Dennis Schulz article, "Angel of Mafraq," *Qantas In-Flight* magazine, 1991.

The personal loyalty of these "Blood Brothers" continued right up to February of 1996, when Aileen experienced her near-fatal auto accident. She needed many blood transfusions. The doctors in charge of The Medina Hospital, also known as the King Hussein Medical Center, mentioned her need to some of the soldiers in an army division near Annoor Hospital. Eighteen men stepped forward and gave blood for her. She said of this: "In the Arab world, people don't like to give blood; so it touched me, very deeply, to see this instantaneous and overwhelming response to my need."

Aileen says that almost none of the Jordanian Arab people are among the terrorists, and, that only a small minority are fundamentalist extremists who are out to kill the "Infidel Christians" as suggested by the Koran. The loving ministry of Aileen and Eleanor medically and socially opened the hearts of the Jordanians to accept them, which all goes to prove, again, God's Word: "Love never faileth" (1 Cor. 13:8). And, however any of us might feel about the Middle East, politically or theologically, we have to be awed, stunned, by what God has done through these two intrepid ladies. They have succeeded in "becoming all things to all men, so that by all possible means, they might save some" (1 Cor. 9:22).

Aileen's deep love for her Bedouin friends is both nontraditional and unconditional. And whether she's treading the dusty deserts, sleeping unknowingly with the rats, blending her blood with the Bedouin men, or eating sheep's eyes, she has faithfully fulfilled the task of adjusting and trusting as she obeys God's call to the marvelously mysterious Middle East.

Mobile Clinic used at Ras A Naqab to travel out into the desert to minister to the Bedouins in their tents, Aileen and Eleanor with a Bedouin Sheik

More testing for TB

Princess Zein and daughter, Zwein, with Aileen visiting a Bedouin tent (1990)

Chapter Six

The God Who Yet Speaks

Aileen and Eleanor built their ministry more on the concept of seeking and finding that one lost sheep rather than looking for the ninety-and-nine (Matt. 18:12-14). Aileen said, "In many circles our ministry would not be considered a success story, but in obedience to the Father, we have sought that one lost sheep."

God has laid a completely unique and peculiar call on the heart of his servant. It is rare to discover many others who have a similar call. It is as though God reminded her that He had not only made remarkable promises to the children of Abraham through the line of Isaac and Jacob, but that He also made great promises to Ishmael and his progeny. This longing to see the children of Abraham, through Ishmael, come to a full knowledge of Jesus Christ, is what makes her call so special. The following poem, by Faye Inchfawn, was circulated amongst prayer societies of London, England, in the 1920s. It presents a viewpoint rarely known in our day, but magnificently expressed in the lives of Aileen Coleman and Eleanor Soltau.

Abraham and Ishmael

by

Faye Inchfawn

How often when the tent is warm at night
And Sarah's eyes are gay,
When Isaac child of laughter and delight
Shouts in his play, dancing with glee
Across the sandy floor, my heart goes to the door,
Following, Oh, the long and weary trail,
My other son, Ishmael.

When er'r they brought new bread
Instantly my heart said, 'Is he hungry?'
When joy in any guise comes near me, then
I say, 'How fares Ishmael today?'

Isaac's a friendly lad, shepherds and herdsmen
Press to do his bidding, glad to serve him,
And Ishmael was at war with every man.
We have great peace without him.
Peace, and yet I never once forget.
Lord God, who made my home so blest;
Lord God, who made my fold both safe and wide;
Father of mercies, wouldst Thou have me rest
While Ishmael's outside?

There are still those who cannot rest because Ishmael is still outside. Such is the call that has been laid in the heart of Aileen Coleman. She really cares, and cares deeply, about the Bedouin people. These children of Ishmael have a hard way of life. And, being a woman, she especially feels for the woman's lot, which is by far the hardest of all. But, remarkably, the Bedouin woman accepts her life as it is, without complaint and without bitterness. Part of the great respect that Aileen has developed for the women has come from observing this high tolerance of suffering and gracious acceptance of the grinding circumstances of her day to day existence. Her day is consumed with simply surviving. The following free verse poem was put in the hands of Aileen Coleman by a Muslim lady from Pakistan who had personally experienced this "journey" before she found new life in Christ.

The Journey

The journey of my life
Begins at home,
Ends at the graveyard.
My life is spent
Like a corpse,
Carried on the shoulders of my father and brother,
Husband and son.
Bathed in religion,
Attired in custom,
And buried in a grave of ignorance.

The Bedouins move seasonally. It's not that they are in a different place every night, which I used to imagine, but it's still very much a nomadic existence. Often she has to carry water long distances from a spring or a well; she can't easily turn on a faucet like we can. So, even though the government does drill some wells to facilitate the watering of the sheep, donkeys, and camels, and for their basic necessities, there is not an abundance. Understandably, they do not use a lot of water for laundry or personal hygiene, because this is of much less importance in the Bedouin world. Just having enough water to drink is the main problem.

Along this line it is interesting to note that, after returning to Mafraq from a visit to the States, Aileen wrote, "Now I am back in Mafraq. The smell of exotic French perfume on women, in meetings in America, has been replaced by the smell of unwashed bodies and wet babies. To me, this is the smell of home. I'm glad to be back doing what God has called me to do."

Having sons is a very important part of a Bedouin woman's life. She is married in her early teens and begins having babies immediately. On occasion, a woman who is unable to have children, or who has only girls, will be divorced by her husband. This is easily accomplished in this primitive culture by a clapping of the hands and declaring her divorced. She has no recourse but to return to the home of her eldest brother. If the husband has some feelings of affection for the barren wife, he may keep her in the household and bring in another, younger wife who, it is hoped, will provide the sons desired by the husband.

Having male offspring is of utmost importance because the sons represent security for the aging parents. It is the acknowledged obligation of the sons to care for the elderly parents when they can no longer care for themselves. When a woman is divorced by her husband, she does not return to her parents, even though they may be capable of caring for her needs. As stated previously, she goes to the household of the elder brother.

Because of this tradition of going for refuge to the elder brother, the gospel is brought into the Bedouin understanding with greater ease. "When I read to them from Romans 8:29b, about Jesus Christ being our Elder Brother," Aileen said, "it makes sense to them that He would be the ultimate place of refuge! When I read Romans 8:29 from the Arabic, the literal translation reads: '. . . the Son of God who is the firstborn of many brothers . . .' In the culture here that is so meaningful because of the privileges and responsibilities of the firstborn son towards the rest of his siblings. Female patients will always give their elder brother's name as the next of kin, not their husband's and usually not their father's."

Bedouin women are, for the most part, illiterate. However, for the last few years there have been schools for Bedouin girls near some of the tribal areas. Although the majority of them are uneducated, they are very intelligent women who have adapted amazingly well to this very difficult lifestyle.

When a Bedouin woman comes to the Mafraq Sanitorium this usually requires a long hospital stay. It's especially difficult for her because it means several months of being separated from her family and children. This presents many different kinds of fear. Uppermost is the real possibility that she will return home to find a new wife in the tent. In her long absence, the husband will have sought another wife to care for the kids, the preparation of the meals, the fetching of the water, and general assistance in the multitudinous chores called for in holding the home together, not to mention the comfort of marital relations which ceased when the first wife left for the hospital.

I know I've been raised in the Western world in an entirely different culture, but I can't help but feel that any woman would be devastated, regardless of her cultural background. Consider what this would do to anyone's sense of self-worth and self-esteem. It almost reduces one to the level of a workhorse; the horse goes lame, so you go get a new horse to do the work.

I asked Aileen why it was necessary, in this day and age, to keep their patients in the hospital for so long. In the States, most cases can be successfully treated with drugs on an outpatient basis. Also, there has been a real reduction in the number of TB cases in America for about twenty years. (However, because of the AIDS epidemic, TB is on the rise again.) Her response to my query explained their position: "There is now a worldwide program trying to control the increasing numbers of TB patients which has been organized by the World Health Organization. In their plan, patients are given their medication under direct supervision of the health worker. This is done on an outpatient basis, where possible. In our case, the situation requires a different procedure, for many reasons: We find it more suitable to have them in the hospital for at least two months of treatment so that we can educate them about their disease. This results in far better compliance to following the treatment prescribed for them. Otherwise, in all probability they wouldn't even follow through on taking the drugs necessary for their healing. Another reason is that most of them have had to travel so far to come to the hospital, that it's almost impossible to follow-up on their progress. Add to this the fact that they're usually malnourished and seldom have enough water to stay healthfully clean."

Upon mentioning the matter of staying clean, Aileen burst into laughter. She said, "I was just remembering a case that was hilarious and tragic at the same time. A few years ago we diagnosed an old man with advanced tuberculosis. We were planning to admit him for treatment, but when he realized he would be required to take a bath, he fled. He hadn't bathed in years. Because of his nomadic lifestyle, we lost contact with him. Now, just recently, we found to our dismay a family of seven, all suffering from tuberculosis. Investigation revealed that they were grandchildren of this old man. He died from the disease, but left a legacy of TB for all his family living in the tent. Six members of this family came to the hospital for treatment and they are all now on the way to health."

"TB spreads like wildfire because these large extended families often sleep under one communal blanket, so that a single coughing carrier can place a whole family at risk."* Aileen, and her fellow-healers face this

---

*"Angel of Mafraq," *Qantas In-Flight* magazine, 1991, by Dennis Shulz.

critical TB crisis daily. They have saved thousands of lives, using their inpatient procedure for forty-three years.

This lengthy hospitalization has a positive spiritual and emotional healing side as well. It provides a wonderful opportunity for Aileen and the hospital staff to really get to know their patients at a much deeper level, as well as providing the patients the opportunity to get to know and trust the staff. Aileen said that as the women begin to feel truly loved, they slowly start to share their problems, the joys, and the heartbreaks that life has dealt to them. It's often the very first time in their lives that they have ever been given any personal attention or have been touched tenderly with loving care. When this happens they are so responsive and so genuinely appreciative. It gives Aileen the chance to become an "elder sister" to them. She has found that it has been a truly beneficial means of breaking down barriers, so that when she does introduce them to "The One she loves," their hearts are more open to hear. Then they are not simply listening out of politeness, but because they have been shown how much she loves them, and how she longs for them to know how much more God loves them and that He has made a way of salvation available to all.

One would think that, because of the tremendous adversity in these women's lives, they would reach out more readily to accept the gospel than the men. But, this has not been found to be the case. The men seem to respond much more quickly, and more often, than the women. Why would this be so? Perhaps because the woman so seldom makes the final decision on any matters of importance. She doubts whether she has the right to make such a decision without male approval. Another possibility is that, due to the harsh treatment she has received and the devaluation of her person because of her gender, she is convinced that such good news could not possibly be for her, but only for men. Convinced of her worthlessness and the presentation of God as masculine in His self-revelation, it would be easy for a woman to assume that she is not worth saving—utterly hopeless.

This brings up in me a well of appreciation for having been born in a nation whose historical origins were rooted and grounded in biblical truth, regardless of how much it has departed from those roots in recent years. The God who honored all womankind forever, by being born of a woman, is revealed in the Gospels. Jesus' attitude toward women accorded to them an equivalent dignity that was revolutionary in its contrast to the times in which He was born. In His resurrection glory, He showed Himself alive to Mary Magdalene, commissioning her first to ". . . go tell My brethren" (John 20:17). The empty tomb was first seen by other women who went there to lovingly anoint His body for burial. To these women was given the first Angelic announcement: "Why seek you the Living among the dead? He is risen" (Luke 24:5-8). The fact that the disciples, (all men), rejected this startling announcement of the women as "idle tales" is evidence of the barriers Jesus was shattering. I, and all women, are the beneficiaries of this incontrovertible historical fact. The usefulness to our Lord of Aileen and Eleanor shows He is still speaking to His brethren from women who "have seen the Lord."

In spite of the fact that Bedouin men might be more open to receive the Gospel message and in spite of the fact that the present plight of the women seems insurmountably difficult, I want to share one of the sweetest stories I've ever heard. It demonstrates so powerfully that God is still able to overwhelm the prevailing culture in His ability and desire to reveal Himself to women.

I'll let Aileen tell you this story in her own words:

"So often I've found that God speaks to these women through incidents in their own lives. He does it so eloquently, so much better than we can, because however long we are there, we'll always think 'western.'

"I remember one lady who had a sterility problem. We were able to help her through treatments, and eventually God gave her a son. For the whole nine months we were treating her, we were sharing the Word with her. We were so sure she'd accept God's way of salvation. She didn't. We were delighted when her son was born. We thought, 'Now will be the time when this lady will realize the wonder of knowing her sins are really forgiven.' She didn't.

"About two years later I heard that the little boy, the son we'd prayed for so much, the one that we'd taken such good care of in infancy, had suddenly died from some desert-related illness. We were also informed that the mother was inconsolable in her grief.

"So, with great trepidation, I went out to her tent in the desert to visit her. Never having been a mother, and never having lost a child, I didn't know what I could possibly say to her. But I just joined this bereaved Bedouin lady as she was sitting alone by her tent. We simply sat there on the ground, this cold winter day and cried together. I began telling her that her son was in heaven. She didn't want her son in heaven; she wanted her son in her arms. She was understandably overwhelmed by her grief. She had not had another son, so this made her situation even more unbearable.

"As we continued to sit silently by her tent, we began watching one of the shepherds as he was leading in a small flock of sheep, with several little lambs. Nearby was a tiny creek of fast-flowing water, perhaps two yards wide, the result of a rare, recent rain. The shepherd simply could not get the obstinate sheep to cross over this fast-flowing water, in spite of the fact that at its deepest point, it couldn't have been more than three or four inches deep. We continued to watch as he pushed them, cursed them, tried to drag them and lead them—all to no avail. The sheep continued to balk. They would not cross the flowing water. Finally, in utter frustration, the shepherd picked up one of the little lambs by the front legs and carried it across the tiny stream of flowing water, putting it inside the tent. With that, of course, the mother of this lamb immediately followed her baby. And, as dumb as sheep are, they all followed that lead sheep across the flowing water into the tent, into their shelter for the night.

"This mourning mother's sobbing had slightly subsided as she soberly sat there, watching this dull little drama. Then, all of a sudden, she began weeping more violently than ever before. I was surprised by this renewed outburst, and said to her, 'Why are you crying?' She said, 'I want you to know that just now God spoke to me.' I asked, 'What did He say?' She replied, 'You know, for a long time you have been telling me I need to come to God in His way, through His Son. I didn't want to. So, God had to take my little lamb across the fast-flowing water of life into Heaven, in order that I would want to be with him badly enough to come to God His Way.' And through her continuing tears she inquired, 'Tell me again. What is God's Way? I want to be sure to be in Heaven with God and with my little lamb.' So with a few simple words I reminded her of God's way: That Jesus had died on the cross in her place, so that by believing in Him she could live forever with God's Son, and with her son."

I must admit a lump comes to my throat every time I recall this painful, poignant story. What an extraordinary revelation God gave to this little heartbroken Bedouin woman, sitting in the dirt beside her humble tent, weeping, somewhere in a lonely desert. What this experience says to me goes down into the very core of my being. It is true, ". . . His eyes range throughout the earth . . ." (Ps. 33:13-14). He truly does know ". . . when even a sparrow falls . . ." (Matt. 10:29). And, it is true that He wants us ". . . to cast all our cares upon Him because He truly cares for us" (1 Pet. 5:7). And, it's true that ". . . the very hairs of our head are numbered!" (Matt. 10:30). And, it's true, ". . . He is no respecter of persons . . ." (Acts 10:34). He loves each one of us the same—enough to die for us personally (John 3:16). And, it is true that all these things are possible because "He lives, He truly lives!" (Heb. 7:25).

God is still bringing the children of Ishmael back into the warmth of Abraham's tent. For, "we are all Abraham's seed through faith in Jesus Christ" (Gal. 3:29). How much God must be rejoicing over that "one little lost lady sheep." What sweet simplicity. What stunning symbolism. What a tender touch of love from our Personal Parent,

The God Who Yet Speaks

"The Lord is my shepherd; I shall not want . . .
He leadeth me beside the still waters.
He restoreth my soul"
(Ps. 23:1, 2b, 3a).

Photo by Dennis Schulz

Beautiful Bedouin Girl

Chapter Seven

Those Little Black Dots

In 1990, when Eleanor and Aileen were both feeling stretched to capacity in their daily work, they were visited by Princess Zein. She presented them with a marvelous challenge. There was, she said, a terrific need for medical care—a diagnostic clinic—in the south of Jordan. The Bedouins there are particularly poor. They're not even able to afford the ten dollar bus fare to the hospital in Mafraq, which is about 185 miles to the north, so most of them are never able to receive proper diagnosis or treatment.

At first, although they were strongly drawn to the idea, they felt it might be more than they could handle. But Eleanor, who was then seventy-four, what is usually considered retirement age, was profoundly moved by Princess Zein's proposition. The more she heard, the more excited she became about fulfilling that great need. Eleanor's mind was "off and running," mentally establishing a diagnostic center for the Bedouins in the south of Jordan. For her there was no "quittin' time." With this fresh vision she was stirred again by the Word of God: "Those who hope in the Lord will renew their strength. They will soar on wings like eagles; they will run and not grow weary, they will walk and not faint" (Isa. 40:31).

When Princess Zein knew that Eleanor was so enthusiastically ready to embark on this latest venture, she set about looking for a possible location. She found a tourist rest stop that was no longer used, owned by the government of Jordan. It was in the tiny village of Ras A Naqab. This is a little village that had been on the main road to the seaport resort town of Aqaba. But because the old road to the Red Sea had been replaced by a newer, more direct route, this tourist stop was no longer needed. So here was this lovely, unused structure, sitting on a mountain-top in the middle of a vast desert, just waiting for them. (Although it had been vandalized, it was completely intact, waiting for restoration.) When they examined the building and saw how perfect it was for their needs, they were really thrilled. After negotiations with the government, they were able to lease this facility for a long term with an amazingly low annual fee. With the help of friends in Australia and America, they were able to completely repair, furnish, and equip the clinic.

The view from the veranda is breathtakingly magnificent. The clinic is situated on the very top of a mile-high mountain, with a south, south-westerly view of over 180 degrees. Below is the barren, rock-strewn desert floor, providing an overwhelming vista, stretching miles and miles in every direction, with distant mountains on the far horizon. Rocks and rocky mountains are as far as the eye can see. (As a master traveler and guide to this whole area, Roy Gustafson, said, "There are ten rocks for every one dirt.") On our recent tour, I had the privilege of standing on that veranda with Aileen and Eleanor and devouring the spectacular beauty of that vast and lonely scene. As we stood there scanning that startling panorama of arid wastelands in all of their utterly isolated, deserted barrenness, Eleanor said to me: "Do you see anything, anywhere, other than rocks and sand?" My response was a quick, "No." Then she handed me her binoculars, and said, "Now take a look." As I adjusted the binoculars, and brought the desert floor into focus, I couldn't believe my eyes. There were scores of little black dots that came into view. Each black dot represented a Bedouin tent. These ancient nomads were scattered all over the entire valley floor right beneath the clinic. Those black-dotted fields were truly "white unto the harvest" (John 4:35). As I viewed this marvel, my heart murmured to my mind, "Isn't it wonderful that God doesn't ever need binoculars." "Nothing in all Creation is hidden from His sight" (Heb. 4:13a).

On this magnificent mountain, there is now a very simple, but adequate diagnostic center, with x-ray and laboratory facilities. There is also a large room where Dr. Soltau and the nurse practitioner interview and examine the patients, a small apartment for the "Doctorah," and a guest room and bath, plus a lovely kitchen and dining area. One small house, quite nearby on the property, has been renovated and provides a home for the nurse and her husband, who takes care of the maintenance and repair of the entire facility.

There was also an old police post quite near the clinic in Ras A Naqab, that had not been used by the police force for many years. It was a beautiful old building with walls about fifteen inches thick, providing ideal insulation. Its architecture was an attractive old Arab style, complete with a courtyard, a stable for horses, and rooms for the officers to live in. It, too, was empty, and again, through the invaluable help of Princess Zein, they were able to lease this building from the Jordanian Police. A work crew from Australia brought their tools with them and did the main repair work on this structure. They renovated it to provide a workshop for maintenance of the entire facility and much needed storage space for supplies and equipment. The residential rooms have been readied for volunteer ministry teams and work crews that come to serve the Lord in Ras A Naqab.

Aileen said, "A friend gave us fifty apple trees, and we planted them, with other fruit trees, all around the former police post. Local kids eat most of the fruit, and what is left we take back to the hospital in Mafraq for the patients."

God has also provided them with a mobile clinic so they can drive to the tribes that are too far away to come to them. This gives them access to the Bedouins who might not even know about the clinic. Eleanor is able to treat as many as fifty patients a day when she travels to them. (Aileen could only join her for two days a week, at most, because her work at Mafraq Hospital kept her so busy.) When they travel to the tribes in the desert, they can diagnose and treat their diseases as well as possible. For the cases that are too serious, they use the mobile clinic, and sometimes their own cars, to transport the patients the 185 miles north to the Mafraq Hospital.

At the official opening ceremony for the Ras A Naqab Clinic many Jordanian dignitaries were in attendance, including Princess Sarvath and Princess Zein, who participated in the ceremonies.

Unlike the Western world, the Bedouins and Arabs have a great regard for old age and gray hair. Add to Eleanor's gray hair and age the incredible regard the people of the desert have for the "Doctorah Soltau" all across the length and breadth of the entire Arabic lands, and you can understand the vast outreach she has from the clinic. And it happened in no time at all. Once the knowledge of her presence on the mountain-top became common, she had visitors from all levels of the culture. Sheikhs would come for social calls to have tea with her and bring ill tribesmen for treatment in the clinic. But, of course, most of her patients were from the poor and needy. Almost at once she was treating twelve to thirteen patients a day. This kept her very busy, for she had to do all the lab work and the x-rays herself. Out in the mobile clinic she can treat far more, but at a less thorough level. Considering her advanced years, her work load is phenomenal.

Recalling their meager beginnings in 1965, it is astounding to realize that these two women now have an outreach of mercy and evangelism that stretches from the border of Saudi Arabia in the south to the border of Syria in the north, to Israel in the west, and to Iraq in the east. Factor in the Bedouin disregard for political borders when they decide to trek, and there are no boundaries to contain the love of God which they have unleashed in the region. Without their active concern there would be virtually no medical aid to reach these people. It is heartwarming to know that God is caring for all those 'little black dots' scattered across the desert floor, and that He has always seen and loved them. Now His two special servants, Aileen and Eleanor, have brought that love and merciful concern to them "in person."

Those Little Black Dots

"... and Jesus said,
'I have other sheep that are not of this sheep pen.
I must bring them also.
They, too, will listen to My Voice,
and there shall be one flock and One Shepherd' "
(John 10:16).

Bedouin tent

Aileen giving a speech at the opening

Ras A Naqab, a mile above sea level, during a snow storm

Chapter Eight

Wars and Rumors of Wars

One day while Aileen was visiting us in our home, our discussion turned to the various tribes among the Bedouin roaming over the desert expanse of the entire Middle East. Struck by the vast knowledge she displayed about a number of the tribes and their histories, groups that lived far beyond the borders of Jordan, I asked her, "How is it you know so much about these various nomads, their histories, and their customs, plus their geographical territories?" She casually replied, "Sir John Glubb taught me." My husband literally exploded, "You knew Glubb Pasha?" She responded, "We had an extended correspondence and chatted on the phone once when I was in England. He's the one who taught me most of what I know about the Bedouin." My husband, a World War II Navy carrier-based fighter pilot, and casual student of military history, pressed on: "Why didn't you ever tell us before that you knew Glubb Pasha?" "Because you never asked," she said, with an amused smile. For me, the name had a vague familiarity to it. I was curious to know what was so exciting about Aileen's tutor.

From its earliest recorded history until this very hour the Middle East has been bathed in bloodshed: "wars and rumors of wars," to use the words of the Lord Jesus Christ. Being the "land bridge" between Africa, Europe, and the Near East, armies from every direction fought across the length and breadth of modern day Jordan, Israel, Syria, Iraq, and Lebanon. During these centuries the ancient nomadic tribes of the desert, the Bedouin, would side with, or fight against, the invaders. This would frequently pit one tribe against the other, and hostilities were communicated from one generation to the other. Since there was no unity amongst these clans, the old "divide and conquer" ploy was used against them, and they were exploited to the advantage of foreigners and victimized by their own ancient hatreds.

Most of us have seen the remarkable David Lean film, *Lawrence of Arabia.* It is the story of the eccentric English Army officer who, for the first time, was able to bring enough temporary unity to the various tribes to assist the British in the defeat of the Turks in 1918. Field Marshall Edmund Allenby was the British General who masterminded the ouster of the Turks. Major John Glubb had served under the command of General Allenby. In the postwar division of the Middle East, Jordan, then Trans-Jordan, had been put under the rule of King Abdullah, the head of the Hashemite tribe. He selected John Glubb to form the Jordanian Army (later to be known as the Arab Legion) and made him a general. The all-Bedouin Army, which he trained, is to this day one of the fiercest fighting forces in the entire Arab world.

In 1947, when King Abdullah was assassinated while entering the El Aksa Mosque on the Temple Mount in Jerusalem, his grandson, Hussein (the present King of Jordan) was named to succeed him. Hussein was only 17-years-old at the time and attending Sandhurst in England. Sandhurst is the English equivalent of our Military Academy at West Point. Upon his graduation and return to Jordan, the young king inquired of Sir John Glubb (by then known affectionately as Glubb Pasha) when he intended to turn the military entirely over to Jordanian command. When he discovered that the general had made no plans to do that, he, after much deliberation, dismissed Glubb Pasha and put the Jordanian military completely under Jordanian leadership. Many years after this wise and courageous decision, an interviewer commended the king for his decision. He turned the compliment aside, saying that it was the brilliance of those who took over the military leadership that had justified the risk.

It was after he was dismissed that Aileen started her correspondence and connection with Sir John Glubb. When she suggested to him that he write a book about the various Arab tribes he responded, "If I were to write a book on growing roses, or a guided coach tour of England, I would have an avid readership. But who, besides you, would read a book on the Bedouin tribes." In his voluminous response, he laid before Aileen a hand-drawn map of the Bedouin world, placing each tribe within the confines of their treks, and in the letters that followed, he shared with her his vast personal knowledge of the various groups. When I asked Aileen where this precious correspondence was, she indicated, sadly, that she had loaned it to a missionary who had lost it.

How fascinating, though, that information gleaned to be used in the training of an army for war should be used, ultimately, for healing and life eternal. Such is the amazing providence of God.

Also, from the prominence of the veranda at the clinic at Ras A Naqab, one looks out into that far distant terrain where Lawrence of Arabia accomplished one his most daring endeavors. It was there that his united tribes attacked a train headed north, loaded with Turkish soldiers. This scene is horrifyingly portrayed in the movie *Lawrence of Arabia* with Lawrence prancing along the top of the wrecked train and glorying in the carnage he had wrought. This bloody victory, however, helped immeasurably in bringing the ultimate victory to General Allenby, ending the oppressive rule of the Ottoman Turks in the Middle East. That was 1918, but in parts of that region, conflicts have continued to rage, with very few intervals of general peace. Now Eleanor, Aileen, and their mobile clinic are moving about in that same desert, visiting all those "little black dots," bringing healing, hope, and eternal peace with God.

Hardly two years after moving to Mafraq in 1965, they found themselves in the midst of the Six-Day War with bullets, bombs, and rockets being fired directly over the hospital at a nearby air base. This was Aileen's first taste of war. "The Israeli jet fighters struck the neighboring base, destroying every plane before they could get airborne. Then they began strafing the Jordanian troops outside her hospital gates, performing a quick barrel-roll over the institution, and, with incredible precision, blasting away at the troops on the other side of the hospital."*

Aileen said, "The hardest thing to bear, in the 1967 war, was the awful noise of the dog fights, when the Israeli planes were intercepted by the few Jordanian planes that were not destroyed on the ground. The screaming of the bombs and antiaircraft artillery was frightening. The terror of the children in the district was both understandable and heart-rending. The distress of the families, when the agonizing news came back, that sons and fathers had been killed in the fighting, made us realize once again the feckless futility of war. It's so useless and so costly. No one ever

*Dennis Schulz

really wins in a war. The grief and anguish seemed to be never-ending; every day meant we were visiting yet another bereaved family." War always affects the already difficult living conditions of the Bedouin, too. It shuts down borders and minimizes usable grazing land for their animals, so malnutrition rages. Sometimes the people become so poor they can't even weave tents. Aileen has seen cases of people living under trees and in caves.

She treated one woman who came to the hospital weighing barely sixty pounds. She looked 80-years-old and was only thirty. I asked Aileen if the Bedouins have guns in their tents, and she said: "Yes, all the men carry arms. Often it is to protect their flocks from foxes, wolves, and hyenas, but, of course, they would not hesitate to use them in self defense, if they felt threatened by human enemies. Because many of them are not living in tents now, a fair percentage of the Bedouin Army is recruited from Bedouin villages."

The next war they experienced was the Black September Civil War of 1970. Once again, when Aileen and Eleanor were told to leave the country, they refused. This time they were occupied by the P.L.O., who were escaping from the Jordanian troops trying to force them into Lebanon. This particular war crisis created a dark-comedy sequence that I still can't quite believe occurred. Aileen related: "When the terrorists (the P.L.O.) roughed us up and stole our cars (you don't argue when you're staring into the muzzle of a gun), I heckled them almost every day, trying to get our cars back. We were practically immobilized without any transportation. (We were still located in our first, small hospital, in the village of Mafraq at this time.) I kept badgering them, and all I got were promises, but no vehicles. Amazingly, however, my frequent visits to their headquarters somehow succeeded in building up a sort of strange relationship with them, although I certainly didn't agree with their position or actions. As a matter of fact, I had great disdain for everything that the P.L.O. represented. I am fiercely loyal to His Majesty, King Hussein. But I recognized the fact that some of the younger ones joined the commandos because it was the 'cool' thing to do—or because of peer pressure. Finally, in frustration, I grabbed one of the Abu Nidal (P.L.O.) leaders, shook my finger at him, like his strict mother, and said: 'You guys stole our cars, so now you're going to have to do our grocery shopping for us.' Would you believe they did it? I demanded and got one of them to come every day, with a handcart, and go to the market, looking for fruits and vegetables for outpatients in the hospital. And they soon learned it wasn't good to bring me inferior food, because if they did, I made them trundle it right back and bring me better stuff. I don't know where they found it, but they were soon bringing us fruits and veggies of far better quality than those offered in the market. They even delivered dinner to Lester, who was working on construction of our new hospital then, which is about five miles from town."

So here is our feisty Aileen, not only standing up to these fierce, fighting P.L.O. troops, but actually getting them to come back each week to do grocery shopping. What an unexpected, wonderful relationship—a setup only God could have contrived. I can't help but think of Proverbs 16:7, "When a man's ways please the Lord, He maketh even his enemies to be at peace with him."

But there's more to this story. After the fighting was over, they heard that someone had seen the hospital pickup truck (one of the two vehicles stolen) in Syria, just across the Jordanian/Syrian border. Aileen continued, "Because I was the only non-American in the hospital, it was my job, unfortunately, to go to Syria to see if the rumor about our truck was true. (The Americans weren't allowed to enter Syria because of the political situation.) So off I went, slightly fearful about what I might be facing, both enroute and after arriving.

"It was a cold, bleak day. Bereft of any vehicle, I had to go by public transport. The bus I stepped into was old and rickety and had ostrich feathers on the fenders for decoration. I really looked the part of 'Miz Missionary,' with boots and a too-large trenchcoat. To complete this stylish ensemble, I had my head covered in that permanently out-of-date, large Muslim-type scarf. Besides being assured that I was culturally acceptable, being well covered by scarf and coat, this stunning outfit also kept me warm. (The bus was freezing cold because almost all its windows were broken.)

"When we arrived in Syria, some of the children on the bus started to wonder audibly and loudly who I was, why I was there, and where I was going. The driver suddenly stopped the bus. As the blood began to rush out to my fingertips, he proceeded to make a loud speech, after he had swatted some of the kids he thought were being too noisy and too curious. Pointing at me, he said, 'We, in Syria, are so grateful for the Soviet woman who came to Syria, dressed as she is, and even speaking Arabic. She's not like those Western women, who come only as tourists, inappropriately dressed and never speaking a word of Arabic.' Then he thanked me, profusely, for leaving the Soviet Union to live and work in Syria.

"As the blood began receding from my fingertips and returning to its proper place in my body, I breathed a relieved prayer of thanksgiving. I decided that a smile and silence would be my safest reaction, all the while hoping that my Australian passport would remain hidden, and that there wouldn't be any questions asked that would force me to reveal my true identity. Amazingly, I debarked uneventfully.

"Miracle of miracles, I finally found our truck and was able to bring it back to Mafraq. It was quite vandalized, but nonetheless, it was good to have wheels again after ten months without any vehicle at the hospital." Yet another example of God's protection, along with a splendid sense of humor.

Continuing with her remembrances of war experiences, once again, the darkness of despair and devastation is lightened by a humorous incident. She recalled, "At the start of the Gulf War, in 1990, the Jordanian troops surrounded the Mafraq Hospital. They were afraid the Israelis would attack the airfield which was only a short distance from the sanitorium. During this time, there were demonstrations, in the larger cities, against the Western Allies. We have no problems with the national people (the ordinary Jordanian citizens), but we have seen that these demonstrations (instigated by the Palestinian Arabs—the P.L.O.) can often get out of hand. Violence can result very quickly when this happens.

"Because I did not want to be the bearer of bad news to families of our younger ex-patriot staff, I advised them to be sure and get out of the way if they saw a demonstration developing anywhere. I didn't want them to stick around and be targets for those anti-western sentiments.

"One day I had business in Amman, the capital of Jordan, about fifty miles from Mafraq. I was driving down a one-way street, when, suddenly, I saw a large, noisy demonstration not too far ahead of me. I couldn't turn around, so there I was, surrounded and trapped to a stop by an angry crowd shouting, 'Death to all westerners.' I immediately covered my head with a scarf (I wouldn't leave home without one of those), hoping thereby to conceal my foreignness. By this time, all the cars in the street were at a complete standstill and at the mercy of the raging crowds.

"All of a sudden, one of the demonstrators tried to open my car door. I kept trying to close it, but finally was unsuccessful. After a terror filled tugging match, he turned to the crowd and said, 'Who can speak to her in English?' (Obviously, my attempted scarf camouflage had not worked this time.) Until then, I wasn't speaking to them at all. So I asked him in Arabic, 'What do you want to tell me?' He then responded with a friendly smile. 'I just wanted to tell you that your skirt is caught in the door and dragging in the mud. Just let me open your door so you can pull it in.' "

"Arabic is a very wide and colorful language, so you can be sure I pulled out all the stops to thank him as graciously as I possibly could. With great relief and appreciation, I blessed his children, and his unborn grandchildren. I thanked him in every way I knew." Once again, I was cognizant of that endearing defensiveness she had for her Jordanian/Arab friends, as she said: "These people can oftentimes sound and be so aggressive, but underneath that exterior beats a heart of concerned friendliness and gentleness. No wonder we love them."

As for me, I simply, silently thank God for once again protecting my dear friend, Aileen. What a threatening situation He managed to turn into a humorous happening. I know she truly believes, along with the Psalmist—"I trust in You, O Lord . . . My times are in your hands" (Ps. 31:14-15a).

It takes my breath away to recount the many ways, through all these years, that the Lord has brought her through illnesses, accidents, dangers of all kinds, and, yes, wars and rumors of wars.

Chapter Nine

Babies

Aileen has won over the Bedouins, not only because of her fluent Arabic, adaptation to the Arab culture, faithfulness through times of war, and her hospital for TB patients, but also, probably primarily because of her tremendous love, which reaches out in every direction.

Scarcely a night at the hospital goes by that doesn't find her sharing her own small sleeping quarters with some needy little baby. Sometimes it's a temporary sick-stop for an ailing baby, but many times it's for the long haul.

Aileen said, "Even though I've never had any children of my own, it's been a great source of personal enjoyment to have been able to raise nine Bedouin babies. Most of their mothers died in childbirth. Their desperate fathers, who could find no one to care for their newborn babies, would bring them to me, begging for help. The first little girl I had is now 21-years-old, living in Syria, and probably married by now. I've lost contact with her because of the great distance between us. But I had the privilege and joy of having her from birth to a year old." (Any mother or father, knowing how bonded you can be to a baby in a year's time, can't help but realize what ripping experiences these were. And she did it time and again.)

"The next babies we had were from a father who lived near the hospital. He came to me frantically one day, asking me if I could help him. He said his wife had just died in childbirth and had left him with twin boys. I asked him if they were healthy, and he answered, 'Oh yes, they're just fine.' I didn't think I could take care of two, so my cooperative colleague, Dr. Eleanor Soltau, said, 'I'll help you with one of them.' So I told the father to bring the boys to me. Well, I was shocked beyond measure when I saw the condition of these babies. The father had assured me that these boys were healthy. One of them weighed three pounds and the other even less. The smaller one was very frail and terribly ill. And so, fourteen years ago, the saga of Anwar and Munir began. They're still part of our lives to this day." (I've met them, and they're as handsome, charming, and healthy as can be). Aileen continued with their story, "They lived with us for two and a half years. Then we felt they needed a family. We also wanted to remove them from the hospital situation where they were continually being exposed to patients with an infectious disease." (It is an interesting fact that in spite of the highly contagious nature of tuberculosis, not a single staff member has ever contracted the disease. Considering the forty-three years of ministry that has gone on, only the sovereign protection of Almighty God can account for such a record. Eleanor was first infected as a child in Korea, and, as previously mentioned, she was cured after she had surgery in Memphis, Tennessee. One of her lungs was removed at the time. Aileen had TB in nurses' school in Australia, and that original infection broke out again while in Mafraq.)

At the hospital they treat all chronic chest diseases, insulin-dependent, diabetic children, and infant malnutrition. But it was primarily because of the exposure to TB that, prayerfully and painfully, they thought it best to return the twins to the tents. Aileen gratefully reported, "They are being raised by a father and sister-in-law who love them greatly. They give them the best care they know how, and we still have the opportunity to love and minister to these boys as they return for their weekly visits. It has been so satisfying, now that they are in their early teens, to continue their weekly Bible studies with them. They have a great understanding of what it means to be a believer in Jesus Christ. So their names are most appropriate. Anwar means, 'Enlightened by God,' and Munir means, 'More enlightened by God.' It's our prayer that these boys will carry 'The Great Light' to their tribe, their people, as they continue to mature in their faith.

"Nine years ago, Noorah, a 3-day-old little baby girl, entered my life. Her mother had also died in childbirth. (This happens quite often because the Bedouins are so far away from any medical assistance. When the women, who usually give birth in their tents, have any complications, they often die before they can make it to the hospital for care. It's not that they're neglected; it's simply that medical help is too far away to be available to them.) So Noorah came into my life as a tiny, hairless little girl. As a baby, she wasn't beautiful, but her wonderful personality overshadowed what she lacked in beauty. However, she has grown into a perfectly lovely looking young lady and has brought us so much pleasure. When she was a few months old, she became desperately ill. We think it was because of some poisoned food she had eaten that had been unintentionally given to her by some visiting relatives. We were devastated and began calling all our friends, everywhere, to pray for her." (How well I remember getting a phone call from Aileen late one night. She was sobbing, simply heartbroken over Noorah's seemingly hopeless condition. We asked our whole church to pray for her. And, in answer to prayer, God saved her life.)

Aileen gratefully recalled: "We believe she was spared to grow up to know Him. She continues to spend a few days a week with me in the hospital, even though she now has returned to the desert. She lives with her father and a new stepmother, who are both very good to her. Because she continues to return to us, so eagerly and so often, I remember asking her once: 'Why do you like to come visit us so much?' (This means she'll be sleeping on a floor mat next to my bed, and she has only the little patients in the hospital with whom to play.) Her answer was, 'Because you bathe me, love me, hug me, brush my hair, and read me stories, and kiss me before I go to bed at night.' This is something every little girl deserves, but so many of them don't have, as they're growing up in that Spartan life that is theirs in the desert."

Aileen saves a pretty dress for her, right there at the hospital, and each time she returns, her first request is to bathe and don her dress. One of my favorite photographs of Noorah shows her all decked out in her special dress, polishing her nails, with no shoes on. Once again, we're delightfully impressed with the fact that "girls will be girls," no matter what their culture might be.

And, "boys will be boys." One night Aileen had Noorah, Anwar and a brand new little baby all sleeping with her in her small room. During the night Anwar had picked up his mat and had gone right outside to sleep. In the morning Aileen asked him why he had left the room, and he said: "I can't stand all that noise; and besides, that baby smells so bad. And, how come I don't get to sleep closest to your bed anymore?" He was put out because the younger ones had been moved into his place. (Aileen didn't have the heart to tell him that he, too, had been very noisy, and smelled pretty bad as a baby.)

The children adore her, as she does them. She is continually amazed at how well they adapt to the more western life style they are exposed to in the hospital and then, just as easily, revert back to life in the desert. She's especially astounded by the little girls. They sleep on dirt floors in their tents, and when they return to the hospital they immediately go through a magical metamorphosis and become feminine girls. And they adjust admirably to being pampered.

It is deeply moving to observe Aileen's love for all the children in the hospital, as well as those she has personally raised. She doesn't just feed, clothe, nurse, and care for them. She deeply loves them, especially those she has raised from infancy. Inevitably, this calls for great sacrifice when she must return them to the tents, even knowing she will see them again.

You must be wondering, as I did, "how does she find the time to take care of these children and run a sixty bed hospital?" She brushed my question aside, quickly, with: "Well, sometimes it *was* a bit frustrating, and I did often lose a lot of sleep." Then she proceeded to smother that line with: "But what a source of personal pleasure it has always been to me."

I was curious about what an "average" day looked like on her schedule. She said: "As hospital administrator I never have an average day." I did manage to get her to spell out what her daily routine is like, and this is it:

5:00 A.M.—Rises; has personal devotions till 6:30 A.M.
6:30 A.M.—Breakfast and devotions with Jordanian nurses.
7:00 A.M.—Catches up on correspondence.
8:00 A.M.—Works with patients in clinic, examines them and does general diagnostic and treatment of the patients.
1:00 P.M.—Lunch. During the afternoon she prepares for the 6:00 P.M. evening meetings with patients. These meetings take place five nights a week, but she can only devote three afternoons for

preparations. All other afternoons are devoted to administrative responsibilities.

6:00 P.M.—Evangelistic meeting with women patients five nights a week. After the evening meal she does more administrative work i.e., ordering medicines, responding to government correspondence, and writing "thank you" letters to some of their donors whose gifts have come directly to them, instead of the office in Boone, North Carolina, or Australia.

This is what a day should be. But add to that the fact that she must meet all government officials who come to the hospital. (She bemoans the fact that the government seems to major in statistics and making reports, at least a couple of times a week.)

She has to interview all prospective employees.

She must respond to missions who have missionaries delegated to them.

At least one day a week she must travel down to Amman to deal with government officials.

As administrator, she must attend all functions to which they, as a hospital, are invited. (In the three weeks following her last visit to the states, she already attended three different evening dinners in Amman, with ambassadors and national government officials.) The last time I checked she had several appointments with ambassadors of Sweden, Switzerland, and Great Britain. They are all doing reports on what is being done for the Bedouins. Aileen said, "I feel like telling them to 'just do it,' and not write reports about what should be done."

When the new missionary nurses arrive from language school, Aileen will begin their ongoing training to serve in the context of their unique hospital. On top of this she intends to find the time to go back out into the desert to visit the tents of those who have become Christians during their stay in the hospital.

Yet, this woman always manages, somehow, to find the time to take care of one more needy infant when the occasion arises. And she will gladly lose sleep at night caring for, raising, adoring, and finally giving back to the tents a healthy toddler.

What a soft, yet strong, sacrificial surrogate mother she is.

"Anyone who takes care of a little child like this is caring for Me. And whoever cares for Me is caring for God who sent Me. Your care for others is the measure of your greatness" (Luke 9:48, The Living Bible).

Chapter Ten

Homecoming

"Stay always within the boundaries
where God's love can reach and bless you!"
(Jude 1:21a, T.L.B.)

The highlight of the year, according to Aileen, is their annual Christmas party. The drawing power of this event is nothing short of phenomenal. Over two hundred return each Christmas season to participate in this purely Christian celebration.

The guests include former patients, present convalescents, visitors from neighboring villages, and both believers and nonbelievers. Annoor Hospital—The Light—truly shines forth in a special way during this holy season—its beam beckoning to the Bedouins from far and near.

In this Moslem land, when people depart from the hospital, healed in body but not in spirit, they return to a world almost devoid of the compelling love of Christ they have experienced in the hospital. Those that leave the hospital healed in spirit as well as body take Christ with them. But, in either case, they would be missing the warm, loving context that brought them to faith and nurtured it as well. They obviously have a deep longing to return to this haven of hope—a yearning to "stay always within the boundaries where God's love can reach and bless them." This extraordinary annual festivity has been taking place ever since the hospital came into being, and Aileen says it's handled in a very simple way.

First, they have their special Christmas morning worship service, which consists of telling the Christmas story using flannelgraph illustrations. Then they praise God by singing carols and the hymns the patients have learned while in the hospital. Next, one of the missionary staff, very clearly, tells all the guests why they rejoice in the birth of Jesus Christ.

Then they pass out Christmas gifts to one and all. The Bedouin people have so little that the tiny gifts they can give them bring unbelievable joy. The presents usually consist of a scarf for the lady, a pair of socks for the man, and the children, of course, get the things that make most kids happy, worldwide: balloons, candies, and toys.

Following the gift-giving, the traditional Christmas dinner is served. Their "turkey and trimmings" consists of one fabulous feast. Trays four feet in diameter are covered with thin wheat bread, which is covered with an 8 inch depth of rice. Chunks of lamb that have been boiled in a very pungent sauce are placed all over. This sauce is made from goat's cottage cheese that has been sun-dried on the tops of their tents. Then, the whole meal is decorated with parsley and liberally sprinkled with toasted almonds and pine nuts. After expressing gratitude to God for the meal, the guests either sit on the ground around the tray, or they eat standing, with their tray on a table. The meal, of course, is eaten Bedouin style, with the right hand. The hostess, as you may remember, tears off the choice pieces of meat and hands them to the guests. Each tray has that captivating cooked head of the lamb as the center piece. This feast is called "Mansef." Afterward, tea, cookies, and candies are served. It sounds delicious, as long as you're not honored with the sheep's eye.

I'm sure it hasn't escaped your notice that this celebration is a huge undertaking. Usually, by the time I talk to Aileen, it's already Christmas night there. (Mafraq is ten hours "older" than California.) She's understandably exhausted by the effort, but, at the same time, exuberantly happy and refreshed by the experience. All the planning, invitations, package wrapping, cooking, and cleanup that have been done by Aileen and the hospital staff seem to have been forgotten because she has seen her beloved Bedouin made happy by the event. Once again, they have heard the Good News that compels their "Araisa" to demonstrate the love of Christ. Once again they have been deeply touched by that same compelling love coming with such consistency from all the hospital staff.

Often, months later, when Aileen visits the tents of some of those who attended the Christmas celebration, she'll notice that even the colored wrapping paper has been carefully smoothed out, folded up, and taken home to remember Christmas.

In recent years, Samaritan's Purse has sponsored a program called, "Operation Christmas Child." Families in the U.S. and other countries are encouraged to fill up boxes, from shoe-box size on up, to meet the needs of grinding poverty found in many areas of the world. The Annoor Hospital has begun receiving a supply of these each year. Aileen says they are wonderful door-openers when visiting the tents. At Christmas time they take the boxes out in the desert to the needy families. One chilly, rainy day she was distributing boxes, and a mother with five little children approached her. They were all poorly clothed and shivering from the cold. She said she watched in amazement and delight as the children pulled warm garments out of their boxes.

The baby, clothed only in a thin sheet and wrapped in a towel, received a complete outfit, including a zip-up snow suit. Aileen said, "As I observed the deep gratitude of the mother and her children, I could not help but think of a family somewhere else in the world who, nudged by the Spirit of God, purchased such thoughtful and useful gifts, lovingly packed them in a box, and sent them to Samaritan's Purse. Then I thought of the generous people who had given money so that Samaritan's Purse could ship them to us. If only all of those people could have seen what I saw that day, they'd have surely understood, 'Our Father knows what we need even before we ask it.' "

How wonderful it is that God beckons the Bedouin back each year to this "Happy Homecoming" to reassure them, and remind them, that there are always "blessings for those who stay within the boundaries where His love can reach and bless them." And it matters not whether those boundaries are in a hospital, a home, or a heart. God's love is an ever-present present for those who have received His gift.

His "Boundaries of Blessings" beckon to the Bedouins, and woo the whole world at Christmas and always.

Eleanor and Aileen, laborers together for Christ for over 40 years

Chapter Eleven

Home-Going

It was one of those moments when your breath, and time itself, seems to stop; fear takes over in full force, and everything else slips into neutral.

On 21 November 1997, the phone rang again. This time, I didn't answer it; my husband did. I heard him let out a low moan, and say: "Aileen, oh no. It can't be." A long pause, then, "When did it happen? How? . . . Oh, I'm so sorry." He motioned to me to get on another phone. When I lifted the receiver, I heard soul-searing sobbing on the other end of the line—pain that could be felt from thousands of miles away—gripping and gouging at my own heart.

As Aileen fought for control, amidst suffocating silence, my husband, fighting back his own tears, softly said to me: "Eleanor has died as the result of an accidental fire." With a reflection of her anguish in my own voice, I heard myself asking, "Oh, Aileen, how could this be? What happened?" Still fighting her emotions, she said: "We're not sure how it happened; we probably never will be. But we suspect it involved the knocking over of a kerosene space-heater, while she was in the process of lighting it. It happened in the living room of our little guest house where she was staying. It would appear that in her effort to extinguish the flames that had begun to engulf her, she had wisely retrieved a blanket from the bedroom with which to smother the flames, not realizing that it was made of a synthetic fabric that is easily ignited. The fumes from the burning blanket were so toxic, that, as she wrapped it around herself—in hopes of smothering the flames—instead, she was asphyxiated by the acrid fumes. At some point, in this struggle, she had opened the front door, but had not left the house. We presume she returned, intending to extinguish the fire herself."

Aileen's disjointed words of distress continued on: "When I went to look for her, because she had not come to supper, I found her lying on the floor, unconscious, and terribly burned. Lying next to her, and dead, was her beloved Saluki hound, who chose to stay by her side and die with her rather than escape through that open front door."

At the fresh remembrance of the awful, heartbreaking scene, her uncontrollable weeping resumed. The full impact of the tragedy began to hit me like painful pellets shot from a gun. Even the cushioning effects of shock could not keep the numbing news from brutally bombarding me. Eleanor was dead. Burned in a fire. That quickly, Aileen's ministry partner of over forty years, her faithful friend—and God's—who had worked so willingly with her in that arid wilderness, had been taken back to God's bosom. What words could possibly describe the searing pain wracking the heart and mind of Aileen, or minister the comfort I so longed to impart.

After our phone conversation ended, I just sat there in a stupor. I knew I'd heard Aileen's words, but I, somehow, could not comprehend them. I didn't for weeks . . . I'm not sure I have, yet . . . Perhaps I never will . . . Maybe it's not possible. Aileen said that there wasn't a jealous bone in Eleanor's body; she was one of those rare individuals who lived her life so that God alone would get the glory. Courageous Eleanor, this faithful, strong pioneer was gone. We'd never hear her laughter or enjoy her sparkling wit again, not in this life. I might never be able to comprehend it fully, but it was a fact.

The rest of her story was shared with me, by Aileen, at a later time.

Because their hospital was not equipped to treat burns, they rushed Eleanor to the nearest facility, about thirty minutes away, where she lived for another six hours. Someone at the hospital thoughtfully called Princess Zein in Amman. "In a little over an hour," Aileen said, "she was at my side and seldom left me until after the funeral."

During this period, Eleanor, though heavily sedated because of her excruciating pain, regained consciousness for a while. With her own knowledge as a physician of the extent of her burns, she stated emphatically to Aileen, "No heroics, please," thereby indicating that she wanted minimum medical treatment, awaiting the inevitability of her departure. Aileen said, "Although she knew she was dying, she was at perfect peace. I asked her if she would like me to read to her from the Bible, and she said that she would. When I questioned her about what passages she would prefer, she said, 'Read all of it!' She then inquired if Princess Zein was there. I told her 'Yes,' to which she responded, 'Oh dear, all I have to serve her is canned tomato soup.' "

Because Princess Zein remained with Aileen, close by Eleanor's bedside, she watched her die. She was very impressed and impacted by her complete sense of peace. She asked Aileen as they left the hospital, "Was it because of her work, that she died so peacefully?" To which Aileen answered, "No, not primarily. We're not saved because we serve; we serve because we're saved. She had peace with God, through our Lord Jesus Christ (Rom. 5:1). She had peace because she knew she'd already been forgiven for all her sins. Her work was never done to try to receive forgiveness, but because she loved God, and she loved the Bedouin people."

So, not only was her life a testimony to the Moslem Bedouins, but, so, also, was the graceful manner in which she died.

Aileen said the last real contact she had with her was about one hour before she died, when she gave her one of her lovely wide smiles and said, "I'm just fine," and lapsed into unconsciousness.

Aileen was grateful that Eleanor went to heaven while still actively involved in God's work. "She just wasn't made to ever become dependent on people and fade away, mentally and physically," she said. At age eighty-one, she had just been asked to be a consultant for the World Health Program for TB, because she was known as "The Dictionary of Tuberculosis."

The outpouring of love from the Muslims for Eleanor was both overwhelming and heartwarming. Of the five hundred that attended the funeral services, three hundred were Muslims. They came by camel, by bus, and on foot, as well as by car. Many came from as far away as Ras A Naqab, that expensive, long, 185 mile bus trip, to pay tribute to their beloved "Doctorah." Aileen was overcome by that sacrificial symbol of support, love, and respect that those poor Bedouin people showed. They not only made that long trip, but they remained in Mafraq for the three days afterwards, which is the traditional mourning time. (This means they slept anywhere they could—on the ground or in makeshift shelters.) That's lump-in-the-throat-love if I have ever seen it. I'm so touched by their deep desire to honor her. In addition, these were mostly men, which makes it even more remarkable and impressive, considering the subordinate role of women in the Moslem culture.

Princess Zein brought in army bulldozers and troops to clear away a large flat area of land within the hospital compound where the funeral was to be held. Since rain was expected for the day of the funeral, these army engineers erected an enormous Bedouin type tent, large enough to shelter hundreds of mourners from the weather.

The hospital staff was overwhelmed with the outpouring of love from the Muslims. There was one whole page of announcements in the local newspaper, devoted to expressing sympathy and appreciation for her life and service.

Let me share some of their condolences. In a letter of consolation, to Aileen, one very high ranking Jordanian official, Omar Shoter, said: "We, in Jordan, are honored to have had her with us; and now, yet again, she blessed and honored us by choosing to be rested in our country." (Aileen has made the same request for herself.)

Antoine Deeb, one of their Christian Arab friends, wrote this breathtakingly, beautiful expression of his thoughts and deep feelings. He began by quoting Romans 16:12, which in Arabic reads: "She made herself tired in the work of the Lord." Then he added:

"The doctor is dead, but healing will continue . . . You have labored with the devoutness of an apostle; you have shown the heroism of a martyr; you have touched more multitudes by your love than by your genius; therefore the fragrance of your name and labor, Eleanor, shall be our breathing atmosphere. Though your candle was unintentionally extinguished, yet Annoor (The Light), with unbending resolve, will continue to shine. As a friend, you have passed away, but your friendship will linger. Your body is buried, and still here, but your presence is within each of us as the throbbing pulse of our renewed commitment."

What wondrous words from the heart and pen of her beloved Arab friend. Truly, "Apples of gold in pictures of silver . . ." (Prov. 25:11).

I was privileged to see the funeral on the videotape which Aileen brought to me on her last visit. Although, of course, all of it was in Arabic, I was amazed that the language barrier did not prevent me from participating, personally, in the whole service. Its message spoke to all my senses and penetrated deeply into every pore of my being.

The service opened with the scripture, 2 Timothy 4:7-8 (KJV), "I have fought a good fight, I have finished my course, I have kept the faith: Henceforth there is laid up for me a crown of righteousness, which the Lord, the Righteous Judge, shall give me at that day: And not to me only, but unto all them also that love His appearing."

There were beautiful wreaths of flowers sent from many parts of the world. They surrounded her casket and covered her body—all except for her face. She is wearing the traditional Bedouin scarf on her head.

All the Scriptures, messages, and tributes were then given by several Jordanian Christian ministers. In the large Bedouin tent was a sea of faces, filled with tears, sadness, and love. Aileen and Princess Zein sat side-by-side in the front row of the tent. Both were attired in the traditional Bedouin long dresses and head scarf appropriate for mourning, and they were surrounded by government officials, other members of the royal family, and friends from all parts of Jordan. Many people were standing outside the tent. The expected rain never came. The size of the crowd was almost unbelievable.

After the speakers and ministers completed their portion of the program, the most emotion-gripping segment of the service commenced. The Bedouins and all who have attended paraded by Eleanor's casket. The depth of sorrow displayed was painful to observe, as they slowly walked past her body. Some stopped to lovingly kiss her forehead; others stared adoringly as they paused for one last look; two Roman Catholic nuns who were present made the sign of the cross; one woman kissed her entire face—weeping inconsolably; one rearranged Eleanor's scarf, and one man waved at her tenderly, saying good-bye.

Then the pall bearers carried her body to its final resting place nearby. The strains of the "Hallelujah Chorus" blared triumphantly over an antiquated, yet adequate, public address system. It was impossible to miss this message in music that could burst through the boundaries of any language barrier. I could literally feel Christ cutting through the cultures, centuries, and countries with His Song of Salvation to all peoples everywhere—Hallelujah—King of Kings—Lord of Lords. Christ is alive! Eleanor is alive! We can all be alive—in Him!

Only faith in the finished work of Christ has the power to turn that last enemy, dreaded death, into such a triumphant, hopeful "home-going."

Eleanor is buried in the courtyard of the hospital compound, right outside Aileen's room. Her gravestone has this simple Scripture etched on it, "She labored much in the Lord" (Rom. 16:12).

Many days after Eleanor's burial, Aileen planted numerous daffodils, narcissus, and hyacinths on her grave. As she was watering them, a little Bedouin boy, a patient, was watching her. Aileen said to him, "The Doctorah's body is here." And he very hopefully said, "Are you watering her to make her grow again?"

What a precious question, and what a perfect way to end this chapter of a very great lady's life.

John 4:14b (KJV) says, ". . . the water that I shall give [her] shall be in [her] a well of water springing up into everlasting life!"

Aileen said of Eleanor, "She was laid to rest in the hospital olive grove, in the land, and among the people she loved. Their land had become her land, and their home her home. I miss her every minute."

Chapter Twelve

To Be Continued . . .

The best thing about this story is that it's not over when I put my pen down. It is but the beginning of a new chapter in the life of Aileen Coleman. Am I saying this as simply a smooth segue into another stage of her time on earth? By no means. There isn't any way I could possibly express with words how difficult these days have been for her. When she visited us for a while, after Eleanor's funeral, it was agonizing to see her aching emptiness, and the sometimes stoic suffering, caused by this physical severance from her longtime faithful friend and ministry partner. I knew she needed to talk about this sorrow, but I couldn't bear to rouse such wrenching pain to the surface. It seemed wise to let her bring it up at her own pace, sharing what she felt able to bear in the remembering. At one point she said, "Losing Eleanor was like loosing my right arm." On another occasion she added, "As I left Mafraq, this last time, the impact hit me with full force. I looked back at the hospital, as I was departing, and thought; 'When I return, she won't ever be here again. I'll be alone.' "

Imagine, over forty years of working together as a team, in a Moslem land, in faith, facing the insurmountable odds, seeing their Lord work miracle after miracle, bonded in prayer, as they confronted all that should have spelled doom for their efforts, and seeing the Living Christ vindicate their call with His improbable answers, seeing Him show Himself alive to the patients they loved in His Name, healing them in body and spirit, and keeping them in the Way, His Way, rejoicing together as God brought person after person into this ministry to share the burden, imagine experiencing all of this together, and now Eleanor was gone to the Lord, and Aileen was alone.

Although they were so very different in personality, they complemented each other perfectly. They were not co-dependent; they were each God-dependent! Perhaps God was gently conditioning Aileen for this separation with the clinic at Ras A Naqab. For the years that it had been open, Eleanor had lived there while Aileen remained at the hospital in Mafraq. There was the phone, and they could talk almost daily, sharing the activities in each location. And there were the times when Eleanor brought a patient up to the hospital, and would spend the night, or, Aileen would join Eleanor and Princess Zein for one of their forays into the black tents with the mobile clinic. Still, she always knew that Eleanor was but a phone call away. Or if they needed to have a face-to-face conference, or just visit, a short day's journey could accomplish that. But, no longer. Eleanor was beyond the reach of the phone, or any earthly journey. Now Aileen is the remaining half of that powerful pair-for-God. The same sustaining Holy Spirit who led them both to Mafraq continues to heal, hold together, guide, and empower Aileen. It is magnificent to behold.

When it was just about time for her to return to Mafraq after her last visit, I asked her to please write down for me what she was presently thinking and experiencing inside. Her eyes saddened and her shoulders slumped, and she sat there for a long time, gathering her thoughts, perhaps, emotionally bracing herself, and then she finally wrote:

"I have had many speaking visits to Australia and America. Most of them have been alone, leaving Eleanor in Jordan to write the checks, and, generally be available for every contingency.

"Eleanor was planning to come to America early in 1998 to visit and report to supporting churches. Her unexpected and sudden death, in November 1997, interrupted these plans. When it was suggested I take her place, I was sure I couldn't cope emotionally with that challenge. But God spoke to me through His Word, in Joshua 1:5b, 'As I was with Moses, so I will be with you; I will never leave you or forsake you.' He reminded me that even though His servant, Eleanor, was dead,

His work would continue. And as He had been with her, so He would be with me—asking only my obedience to His Word, courage to move forward and strength to believe His promises.

"God helped me get through my busy schedule of speaking, in 1998. And, so I return to Mafraq. Eleanor won't be there enthusiastically waiting a report, laughing at my 'mess-ups,' and rejoicing in what God had done. And we had planned to begin a new ministry in which, together, we would visit former patients in their tents, who had found new life while being treated in the hospital. It is hard for them to thrive without any fellowship or encouragement in their faith. We were sure this was what God was leading us to do.

"Now, I am returning to Jordan—to the country and the people I love—and to the ministry to which God has called me. But I have such a hole in my gut. Eleanor is not there to welcome me.

"I do not believe we were mistaken in our understanding of God's will for us. So I will return and continue, alone, this ministry of visiting the women who love Jesus Christ. My very poor sense of direction convinces my friends that I could get lost in a parking lot. So as I trek the trackless deserts alone, I will be proving more of God's promises: '. . . to make a way in the desert . . .' (Isa. 40:3), which will get me to the desert and back home again to Mafraq."

She's back home now, doing what she has always done; and, yes, she has gone into the desert to visit the believers there; and, yes, she has found her way back home. Is God's hand still on the work? In the most recent newsletter I received from the hospital, Aileen reports: "This week I was examining patients in the clinic, and a very beautiful young Bedouin woman was pleading for admission. She could have been treated as an outpatient, but when I heard her story, I decided admission was preferable. One of her relatives had been in the hospital for several months. When the relative returned to the tribe, she told this young Bedouin woman all she knew and believed about the Gospel, and about the change in her life since she had believed. The young woman told me, 'I must hear for myself, so that I, too, can know the truth about your Savior. That's why I must come in and hear about your faith.' "

"She is in the hospital, full of questions and eager to hear and learn. We pray for her salvation. Then there would be two of them in the tribe who could encourage each other."

Yes, this story is "To be continued . . ."

And if I were allowed only one word to describe my friend, Aileen, it would have to be "courageous." She has shown amazing mettle from her first entrance into the Middle East to this very day.

Courage: To answer God's call, as a young woman—to put Him first in her life.

Courage: To perform that cesarean section by the book in Sharjah.

Courage: To leave Baraka Hospital in Bethlehem and launch out, with one other woman, into a completely male-oriented Muslim world.

Courage: To become Bedouin in every way God's Word allowed.

Courage: To believe God for impossibilities.

Courage: To build a hospital beginning with nothing.

Courage: To eat a sheep's eye, if necessary, to become "all things to all people."

Courage: To raise and love babies she knew she could never keep.

Courage: To keep on keeping on for over forty years.

Courage: To continue the work after Eleanor's death.

Courage: To keep that formidable schedule of work, even though she lives in a body that still cries out for painkillers every day since her car crash two and half years ago.

Lastly, I'm so grateful she's had the *courage* to remain faithful to that initial, humble, day-by-day vision of theirs—to "reach that one lost sheep."

When I asked Aileen what she wanted to have happen with this book, she said, "I want the people to know how wonderful the Bedouin Arabs are, and how much I love them."

I hope I have succeeded in doing that.

Her beloved Bedouins do not know that a book has been written about her life, nor would they care. They have something far better to read: the love of Jesus on the face of this devoted servant of His, Dame Aileen Coleman.

Abraham's tent she longs to fill,
Will ne'er be satisfied
Till each lost sheep ~~~ till every child
Of Ishmael is inside.

An 'Angel of the Desert,'
We can all agree on that.
But, ask her what she calls herself,
It's still the Desert Rat.

Epilogue

The main body of this book was written during the reign of King Hussein. After his much-lamented death, his son, King Abdullah II, succeeded him.

During this time, Aileen has continued her remarkable ministry, overseeing the treatment of an average of fifteen hundred patients a month at the hospital in the north and the clinic in the south. Any concern about the attitude of the new regime has been amazingly laid to rest. In the year 2000, King Abdullah II issued a royal Decree bestowing upon Aileen Coleman the King Hussein Medal of Honor for her continuing service of mercy and healing to the citizens of Jordan.

Since then, a completely new medical mobile unit has been provided for the development of a ministry to the tubercular Bedouin in the northeastern deserts of Jordan. King Abdullah II dedicated this amazing provision for an expansion of their outreach, with an appropriate ceremony in which the mobile unit was put at the disposal of Aileen. Others might take the time to bask in this kind of recognition and celebrity — not so, The Desert Rat. She has relentlessly continued in her ministry of compassion to the Bedouin and others.

For an extended period of time, covering several months, Aileen has been managing the Ras An Naqab Clinic in the south, returning weekly to the hospital in the north to oversee the work there. The necessity of her presence in the south was occasioned by a shortage of personnel which has since been remedied.

But the most significant reminder of the very heart of Aileen's ministry is defined in an e-mail I recently received from her. The subject line read, "I've done it again!" What she was referring to is explained by recent events. Some months back, she wrote, "There is nothing much to add except that I will be taking a 5-day-old baby back to Naqab with me. He is an illegitimate child Nasri and his wife, Menahi, rescued. Actually they rescued the mother from death by her family because of her pregnancy out of wedlock. He is a beautiful baby. Right now he has jaundice, but he'll be lovely when the color fades. I will keep him with me, while Nasri seeks a believing family who will take him as their own. I thought I had given up the baby stuff, but I will probably still be doing it from my wheelchair."

Then, a little later, a letter said of the baby boy, "He's becoming very lovable," which only means that another baby has wrapped himself around her heart. (She cared for this newborn infant while carrying on all of her usual responsibilities.) A subsequent communication indicated that the baby had been placed into the arms of a grateful, childless, Christian Jordanian couple. Little was said about the ripping experience of letting go of another baby with whom her heart had bonded. That's why her most recent e-mail was titled, "I've done it again!"

It continued, "I guess I will never get too old to be a sucker when it comes to babies. But now I have one of a pair of twins. She is called Basimih, which means 'smiling.' This came about because I met a Bedouin grandmother in the market one day, and she told me that her daughter had delivered twins, and that they were living in a tent in the desert. She said that the babies were still in intensive care in the government hospital and wondered if I could help. I immediately said, 'I don't think so.' Then I went and saw the tent where they would be living. It was cold and rainy, and the floor was just mud, with a small camel manure fire in the middle of the floor. So, remembering my warm room where I would keep them, I started to rethink my reluctance to help. Then, ten days ago, the grandmother appeared with the baby girl who had been discharged from the hospital to die. 'She was just a girl,' they said. She weighed less than four pounds and wasn't making any progress there. So, instead of the grandmother taking her home, she came here with her.

That is when the sucker in me said, 'Give her to me.' It has been sort of a struggle keeping her alive, but I think she is going to make it. She is now retaining her food and starting to gain weight slowly. The mother can't come because she is out in the desert with their few scraggly sheep. Basimih is a beautiful little girl."

Yes, she's done it again! And even as you've been reading these words she's been doing it day by day by day by day! Her remarkable story is definitely "To Be Continued."

An 'Angel of the Desert,'
We can all agree on that.
But, ask her what she calls herself,
It's still The Desert Rat.

We welcome comments from our readers. Feel free to write to us at the following address:

Editorial Department
Huntington House Publishers
P.O. Box 53788
Lafayette, LA 70505

or visit our website at:

www.huntingtonhousebooks.com

More Good Books from Huntington House Publishers

E-vangelism

Sharing the Gospel in Cyberspace

by Andrew Careaga

Cyberspace has become a repository for immense spiritual yearning. The Internet is reshaping the way we work, interact, learn, communicate, and even pray. Provided are ideas for building a website and helpful guides for Christians to find their way around the maze of chat rooms, discussion groups, and bulletin boards found on the Internet.

ISBN 1-56384-160-6

Evangelism That Works

by Phil Derstine

Phil Derstine brings a fresh, innovative approach to soul winning, blending biblical truths with eye-opening personal experience. With a plan that is simple but profoundly effective, he teaches you how to share your faith with others. It is his love for people and distinctive burden for souls that have taken him to the streets with the message of hope.

ISBN 1-56384-191-9

Wired to Work

Answering the Two Most Important Questions in Life

by Vince D'Acchioli

Have you ever wondered what God's plan for your life is? Would you be more successful and happy if you were fulfilling your destiny? Vince D'Acchioli helps you discover *how* and *why* God made you and shows that your were **born** to succeed! Stephen Strang, CEO and Founder of Strang Communications Co., says *"So open the toolbox ... and get started. You won't find a more useful resource.* John C. Maxwell, Founder of the Injoy Group, says that *"Vince D'Acchioli has a unique and powerfully effective way of leading men and women to a discovery of God's plan for their life. Don't miss out on the importance of this life changing message."* Vince D'Acchioli is the Founder of On Target Ministries, based in Monument, Colorado, who has over the past few years, conducted seminars, workshops, church services, and Promise Keepers rallies that have impacted people's lives across the U.S. and Canada.

ISBN 1-56384-191-6

Another Look

by R.L. Brandt

Reverend Brandt asks us to ponder and re-examine our most cherished interpretations of Scripture. Every chapter is replete with profoundly penetrating insight — taking *another look* at Faith, Satan, God, Truth, Repentance, Grace, Heaven. As each of us interprets Scripture in the light of our own mind-set, we often see in Scripture what is not there or we miss what is really there. It is therefore imperative that all of us take another look and let the Holy Spirit guide us to the true interpretation.

ISBN 1-56384-183-5

Married

Happily Ever After?

by Dudley Bienvenu, Jr.

Is staying in love for a lifetime and living happily ever after mere fantasy, or is it really possible? There is an epidemic sweeping our country, destroying our marriages and families. It's called divorce. With over fifty percent of all marriages and sixty percent of second marriages now ending in divorce, millions of lives are being affected. *What's missing? What's the answer?* Author Dudley Bienvenu says, *"You can learn how to 'love the one you're with' always and forever."* For almost two decades, Bienvenu has utilized his teaching and counseling gifts in helping to strengthen and restore marriages. Many of the techniques and lessons he uses to help couples are revealed in this book.

ISBN 1-56384-189-4

The Highest Calling ... Fatherhood

by Michael D. Barnes

This unique book explores the biblical approach to the high calling of fatherhood. It is a handy, step-by-step instruction book for fathers who want to teach their children the ways of God. Dr. Joseph Umidi, Professor of Ministry of Regent Divinity School says, *"I am recommending this book to all my pastoral students, my parishioners, and those wanting to know how to 'turn the hearts of the fathers to the children.' This book is full of hope and will breathe life into your situation."*

ISBN 1-56384-186-X

Are We Living In the End Time?

Prophetic Events Destined to Impact Your World

by Rod Hall

b iblical Prophecy and its revelance to our World. What are the prophectic events destined to impact our world? Wars! Famine! Earthquakes! Massive destruction around the globe! From his 30 years of intense research and study of the prophecies of the Bible, the author shows us the many societal trends and world events taking shape today. The Word of God is the foundation of all knowledge, understanding, and hope. It is a guide to living and provides a worldview that will become our future reality.

ISBN 0-933451-48-2

Inside the New Age Nightmare

by Randall Baer

Are your children safe from the New Age movement? This former New Age leader, one of the world's foremost experts in crystals, brings to light the darkest of the darkness that surrounds the New Age movement. The week that Randall Baer's original book was released, he met with a puzzling and untimely death—his car ran off a mountain pass. His death is still regarded as suspicious.

ISBN 0-910311-58-7
Salt Series ISBN 1-56384-022-7

The Cookbook: Health Begins in Him

by Terry Dorian, Ph.D.

The is an action plan for optimal health and hormone balance! *The Cookbook: Health Begins in Him* offers a dietary regime and food preparation based on both scientific studies and biblical guidelines. Under Dr. Dorian's directions, whole-foods chef Rita M. Thomas has created one hundred and seventy recipes with instructions on:

- *How to prepare breads, pastas, cereals, and waffles with freshly milled flour.*
- *How to prepare desserts that help maintain optimal health.*
- *How to prepare raw vegetable dishes, raw vegetable dressings, cooked vegetables, grain-based casseroles, beans and grains, fermented dishes, and soy foods.*

ISBN 1-56384-127-4

ABCs of Globalism

A Vigilant Christians Glossary

by Debra Rae

Do you know what organizations are working together to form a new world order? Unlike any book on today's market, the *ABCs of Globalism* is a single volume reference that belongs in every concerned Christian's home. It allows easy access to over one hundred entries spanning a number of fields–religious, economic, educational, environmental, and more. Each item features an up-to-date overview, coupled with a Biblical perspective.

ISBN 1-56384-140-1

En Route to Global Occupation

A High Ranking Government Liaison Exposes the Secret Agenda for World Unification

by Gary H. Kah

Kah warns that national sovereignty will soon be a thing of the past. Political forces around the world are now cooperating in unprecedented fashion to achieve their goal of uniting the people of this planet under a New World Order. High-ranking government liaison Gary Kah was dismissed from his position when he refused to "keep silent" and warns that national sovereignty will soon be a thing of the past. Invited to join WCPA (World Constitution and Parliamentary Association), the author was involved in the planning and implementation of a one-world government. For the skeptical observer, the material in this should serve as ample evidence that the drive to create a one-world government is for real. Reproductions of the original documentation are included.

ISBN 0-910311-97-8

New World Order

The Ancient Plan of Secret Societies

by William T. Still

For thousands of years, secret societies have cultivated an ancient plan which has powerfully influenced world events. Until now, this secret plan has remained hidden from view. This book presents new evidence that a military take-over of the U.S. was considered by some in the administration of one of our recent presidents. Although averted, the forces behind it remain in secretive positions of power.

ISBN 0-910311-64-1

How to Homeschool (Yes, You!)

SALT SERIES BOOKLET

by Julia To to

Have you considered homeschooling for your children, but you just don't know where to begin? This book is the answer to your prayer. It will cover topics, such as; what's the best curriculum for your children; where to find the right books; if certified teachers teach better than stay-at-home moms; and what to tell your mother-in-law.

ISBN 1-56384-059-6

Anyone Can Homeschool
How to Find What Works for You

by Terry Dorian, Ph.D., and Zan Peters Tyler

Honest, practical, and inspirational, *Anyone Can Homeschool* assesses the latest in homeschool curricula and confirms that there are social as well as academic advantages to home education. Both veteran and novice homeschoolers will gain insight and up-to-date information from this important book.

ISBN 1-56384-095-2

One Year to a College Degree

by Lynette Long & Eileen Hershberger

Anyone who's been through the gauntlet of higher education's administrative red tape can attest to the confusion that accompanies the process. Twenty-eight years after a failed first semester, co-author Eileen hershberger embarked on the admirable, albeit frightening venture, as an adult learner. One year later she earned her bachelor's degree. With Lynette Long, she reveals the secret in this thorough self-help book, complete with reference guide, work sheets, and resource lists. Most intriguing are the inside tips only professors and upper-level counselors would know.

ISBN 1-56384-001-4

Cloning of the American Mind
Eradicating Morality Through Education

by B. K. Eakman

Why are our children having problems learning? Find out what is really happening in our public schools. *Are the various educational programs being touted really helping our children learn? What is electronic profiling? How does psychologically based teaching hurt our children? Is the teacher really qualified to determine that my child needs Ritalin — isn't that a diagnosis for a doctor to decide? Are teachers really being taught to teach the basics that every child should know?* These are just a few questions every parent should be asking our school officials. The research and thorough documentation by the author will open the door to what is really happening to our educational system. What can we as parents do to ensure our children are taught the basics? Check out Chapter 4 — you'll find many tips and suggestions for parents to work with the school establishment (school boards, education committees, legislative, etc.) to combat the programs that don't work. *Cloning of the American Mind* has been described by one radio host as *one of the most comprehensive books on education.* Thomas Sowell, *New York Post (*September 4, 1998 issue) writes that *"Parents who do not realize what a propaganda apparatus the public schools have become should read* Cloning of the American Mind *by B.K. Eakman."*

ISBN 1-56384-147-9

The Myth of ADHD and Other Learning Disabilities
Parenting Without Ritalin

by Dr. Jan Strydom and Susan du Plessis

If your child has been diagnosed with ADHD or some other behavior disorder, be careful. This diagnosis could be false. The authors of this book explain how parents can teach their children the skills of concentration and self-control without drugging them into submission. With over 25 years in education, consultation and research of learning and behavior problems, Dr. Strydom has helped many parents find ways to help their children.

ISBN 1-56384-180-0

The Deadly Deception
Freemasonry Exposed..
By One of Its Top Leaders

by Jim Shaw and Tom McKenny

This is the story of one man's climb to the top, the top of the "Masonic mountain." A climb that uncovered many "secrets" enveloping the popular fraternal order of Freemasonry. Shaw brings to life the truth about Freemasonry, both good and bad, and for the first time ever, reveals the secretive Thirty-Third Degree initiation.

ISBN 0-910311-54-4

The Hidden Dangers of the Rainbow

by Constance Cumbey

This nationwide best-seller paved the way for all other books on the subject of the New Age movement. Constance Cumbey's book reflects years of in-depth and extensive research. She clearly demonstrates the movement's supreme purpose: to subvert our Judeo-Christian foundation and create a one-world order through a complex network of occult organizations. Cumbey details how these various organizations are linked together by common mystical experiences. The author discloses who and where the leaders of this movement are and discusses their secret agenda to destroy our way of life.

ISBN 0-910311-03-X

Spiritual Warfare
The Invisible Invasion

by Thomas R. Horn

Thomas Horn illustrates through fresh and powerful new insights that while demonic activity has frequently been overlooked, the close collaboration between social architects and ancient evil powers has at times allowed demons to control the machine of world governments, and the moral and social trends of a nation.

ISBN 1-56384-129-0

Government by Political Spin

by David J. Turell, M.D.

Political Spin has been raised to a fine art in this country. These highly paid "spin doctors" use sound bites and ambiguous rhetoric to, at best, influence opinions, and at worst, completely mislead the public. *Government by Political Spin* clearly describes the giant PR program used by Washington officials to control the information to American citizens and maintain themselves in power.

ISBN 1-56384-172-X

The Coming Collision
Global Law vs. U.S. Liberties

by James L. Hirsen, Ph.D.

Are Americans' rights being abolished by International Bureaucrats? Global activists have wholeheartedly embraced environmental extremism, international governance, radical feminism, and New Age mysticism with the intention of spreading their philosophies worldwide by using the powerful weight of international law. Noted international and constitutional attorney James L. Hirsen says that a small group of international bureaucrats are devising and implementing a system of world governance that is beginning to adversely and irrevocably affect the lives of everyday Americans.

Paperback ISBN 1-56384-157-6
Hardcover ISBN 1-56384-163-0

Government by Decree
From President to Dictator
Through Executive Orders

by James L. Hirsen, Ph.D.

Could Americans lose their constitutional rights and be forced to live under martial law with the stroke of open? Sound like fiction? Wrong! Right now, through the use of a tool called an executive order, the President of the United States has the power to institute broad, invasive measures that could directly impact the lives of average, everyday Americans. What might trigger the exercise of this type of awesome power? Any number of things could, but for certain, a crisis, real or manufactured, is the most frightening prospect.

ISBN 1-56384-166-5

What Would They Say?
The Founding Fathers on Current Issues
by Glen Gorton

Thomas Jefferson, John Hancock, George Washington — If these men could once again walk through the halls of Congress, surveying the present scene, what would they say? We were told by the Clinton administration that things like honor and integrity don't matter as long as the rate of inflation is kept down. Our Founding Fathers disagree. They believed that high moral character is an essential ingredient of leadership. Into the heated atmosphere of today's social and political crossfire comes a refreshingly new point of view from — the Founding Fathers. This is not another analysis of the men and their times, but rather, the penetrating and concise testimony of America's greatest heroes. Herein lies the strength of this 240 page anthology: the Founding Fathers themselves. *What Would They Say?* is divided into three parts: (1) Part One has quotes under topics covering Character, Patriotism, Federal Power, Crime, Taxes, Education, Gun Control, Welfare, Term Limits, and Religion; (2) Part Two gives the reader an animated and personal glimpse into the life of each of the 28 men quoted; and (3) Part Three contains a copy of the *Declaration of Independence,* the *US Constitution,* and the *Bill of Rights.*

ISBN 1-56384-146-0

Gender Agenda:
Redefining Equality
by Dale O'Leary

All women have the right to choose motherhood as their primary vocation. The radical feminists' movement poses a threat to this right — In the early 1970s, a small group of radical feminists weren't satisfied with equal rights — they wanted to restructure society as a whole. When mainstream women refused to accept the feminist world view, these radical feminists turned to the legislative process to enforce their agenda. And, under the guise of conventions for the rights of women, the United Nations is now actively promoting a radical feminist ideology. In *The Gender Agenda: Redefining Equality,* author Dale O'Leary takes a spirited look at the feminist movement, its influence on legislation, and its subsequent threat to the ideals of family, marriage and motherhood. By shedding light on the destructiveness of the feminist world view, The Gender Agenda exposes the true agenda of the feminist movement.

ISBN 1-56384-122-3

My Genes Made Me Do It
A Scientific Look at Sexual Orientation

by Neil and Briar Whitehead

Is homosexuality biologically fated? If it is, shouldn't gays be allowed to marry? Can gays change their sexual orientation and become heterosexual? What does science really say about homosexuality and sexual orientation? Taking a mainstream scientific position, this clear, comprehensive and accessible book concludes that a close and careful examination of the scientific evidence does not support the current views that homosexuality is genetic, intrinsic, or fixed. Neil and Briar Whitehead have been researching homosexuality for over eight years. Neil is a research scientist with a Ph.D. in biochemistry. Briar is a writer. They have found many people who feel that gays are "born that way" — but few who understand enough about genetics and human biology to mount a thorough defense of the facts.

ISBN 1-56384-165-7

That Kind Can Never Change ... Can They?
One Man's Struggle with His Homosexuality

by Victor J. Adamson

Author Victor Adamson shares this true story of his struggle to understand and then overcome his homosexuality. Was he born this way or was he conditioned by abuse, environment, and circumstances? Could God love him in spite of the lifestyle he was leading? *Was it possible for someone like him to change?* This true story of his path to victory is shared so that others may know that nothing is impossible with God.

ISBN 1-56384-175-4

Liberalism
Fatal Consequences

by W. A. Borst, Ph.D.

Liberalism indicted! *Liberalism: Fatal Consequences* will arm conservatives of all kinds (Christians, Orthodox Jews, patriots, concerned citizens) with the necessary historical and intellectual ammunition to fight the culture war on any front as it exposes the hypocrisy of liberalism.

"...an excellent critical examination of the issues that threaten to divide our nation."

—President Roche, Hillsdale College

ISBN 1-56384-153-3

Pursuing the Permanent

Meeting the Part of You That Lives Forever

by Jayne Reizner

Amidst hectic schedules and fast-track careers, people in modern society spend most of their time focusing on responsibilities at work and home, leaving little energy for spiritual reflection and meditation. In Pursuing the Permanent, author Jane Reizner stresses the importance of nourishing the innermost part of ourselves -- our souls. She addresses pertinent spiritual questions about life, including: *How can I live with an eternal perspective? How can I pursue ordinary, everyday routines with passion? How can I live in harmony with God and others? Pursuing the Permanent* entreats us to ignore society's definition of happiness and instead focus on the needs of our souls. Then, we can learn the secret of living life on earth with an eternal perspective that emanates from the core of our being.

ISBN 1-56384-126-6

101 Biblical Secrets for Success

Financial, Emotional, and Spiritual

by Sherwood Jansen, Esq.

101 Biblical Secrets for Success is comprised of 101 easy-to-read chapters. The author demonstrates that the age-old philosophies from the Old and New Testaments are ever current and applicable to everyday situations. Subjects include: *Secrets to Attaining Happiness, Ways to Health, Keys to Effective Communication, How to Put Passion into Your Work, Cures for Insomnia, The Importance of Money, Prosperity for Your Family, Defeating Discouragement, The Wisdom Found in Women, Time Management, Thinking Thoughts of Greatness.*

ISBN 1-56384-176-2

The Separation of Church and State

Has America Lost Its Moral Compass?

By Stephen Strehle

Can Religion be divorced from politics? Author Stephen Strehle contends that the path of righteousness and moral accountability is the roadway to our nation's prosperity. Our inalienable rights grew out of the western religious tradition of natural law, egalitarianism out of the universal scope of the Christian Gospel, democracy out of the polity of Puritan congregations;, capitalism out of the Protestant work ethic. Human beings cannot live in self-sufficient autonomy. God is over all, in all, and through all.

ISBN **1-56384-180-0**

Fiction

Patriots

Surviving the Coming Collapse

by James Wesley, Rawles

Patriots, a fast-paced novel by James Wesley, Rawles is more than a novel — it's a survival manual. Could you survive a total collapse of civilization — a modern Dark Ages? Would you be prepared for the economic collapse, the looting, riots, panic, and complete breakdown of our infrastructure?

"More than just a novel, this book is filled with tips on how to survive what we all hope isn't coming to America." —Jefferson Adams, *The Idaho Observer*

ISBN 1-56384-155-X

The 3 Loves of Charlie Delaney

by Joey W. Kiser

A delightful story of first love, innocence, heartbreak, and redemption. Kiser uses his pen to charm and enchant but most of all...to remind.

ISBN 0-933451-45-8

A Fruitful Field

by Cliff Schrage, Jr

First-time novelist, Cliff Schrage, takes us from the abyss of heartbreak to the fervor of redemption. A modern novel that brings us a fresh awareness of God's compassion.

ISBN 1-56384-182-7

Heavenly Odyssey

by Judy Bailey

We have all heard or read the stories of those left behind on earth after the rapture. This fictional story based on the Bible gives us a peek into what is happening in heaven to those who left. Travel with Judy Bailey on this heavenly odyssey as her feet touch Heaven's shore. Experience the Marriage Supper of the Lamb, the heart-wrenching cries of the tribulation saints, the horror being played out on earth, and the war in heaven between the Arch-angel Michael and Satan.

ISBN 1-56384-174-6